The proceeds

from the sale of this book go back into the Houston area in the form of projects and grants to a wide variety of groups in our community.

Our current projects are:

HOUSTON MUSEUM OF NATURAL SCIENCE

THE HOSPICE AT THE TEXAS MEDICAL CENTER

TEXAS MEDICAL CENTER PARK

THE MUSEUM OF FINE ARTS, HOUSTON

THE MUSEUM OF FINE ARTS, RIENZI

URBAN HARVEST

*This volume would not be possible without
the generosity of our members who enthusiastically
shared their favorite recipes and the dedication of the
cookbook committee who unselfishly tasted them all!*

bright sky press

2365 Rice Boulevard, Suite 202, Houston, Texas 77005

©2009 The Garden Club of Houston, 4212 San Felipe PMB 486, Houston, Texas 77027-2902

10   9   8   7   6   5   4   3   2   1

Library of Congress Cataloging-in-Publication Data

Seasonal favorites / The Garden Club of Houston Bulb and Plant Mart /
copy and illustrations by Gay Estes, recipes compiled by Karen Terrell
p. cm.
ISBN 978-1-933979-54-0 (softcover with flaps)
1. Cookery. 2. Entertaining. I. Garden Club of Houston. II. Title.

TX714.S426 2009
641.5—dc22   2009025037

Author and Illustrator: Gay Estes
Editor: Karen Terrell
Copy Editor: Kristine Krueger
Designer: Hina Hussain
Book concept design by Tutu Somerville

Printed in China through Asia Pacific Offset

Seasonal Favorites

THE GARDEN CLUB OF HOUSTON **BULB AND PLANT MART**

BRIGHT SKY PRESS

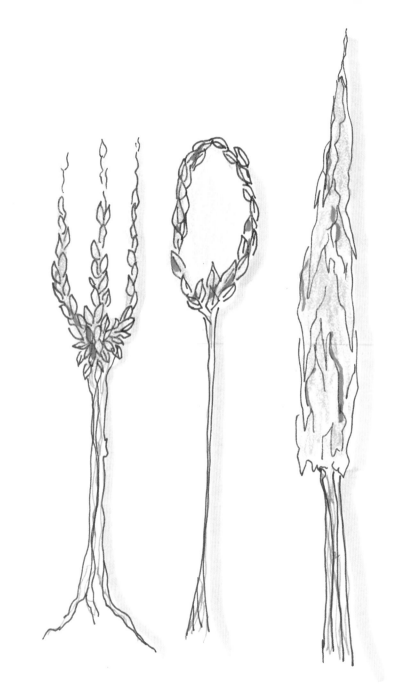

table of
contents

At The Garden Club of Houston, we—as all gardeners do—love living things; we work and play hard to discover beauty and make it part of our gardens, our homes, our kitchens and our planet. In *Seasonal Favorites,* we have compiled tasty tried-and-true recipes, hints from our wonderfully useful Bulb and Plant Mart Culture Sheet, advice from our experts—both horticultural and ecological—and we have tapped the creative spirit of our members to share their favorite holiday and seasonal décor.

As Epicurus said, "The first taste is in the eyes." We have gleaned recipes for entire family feasts and easy shortcuts. Some are simple and some are challenging; all are favorites that we are delighted to share with you. Join us for a journey through the year of gardening, cooking, sowing and reaping.

Seasonal Favorites is a celebration of food, the decoration and presentation of that food, and the special days we set aside for feasts. It is full of the tips that most aid us in providing our own bounty and enjoyment.

As the world turns, the seasons come and go, each bringing special delight to the senses with its own unique treats, celebrations and tasks. Throughout all religions there is an affinity with the earth and its bounty. The Garden of Eden was the biblical setting for mankind, and the story of horticulture is as old as Cain and Abel. Nomadic life chasing game in antiquity morphed to an existence based on cultivation and harvest.

Seasons once held more power over us. Spring has always been full of beautiful flowers, but since it is a time of planting and sowing, it meant near starvation for the settlers in the New World; fall is the time for reaping. We have been cooking what we harvested since the discovery of fire. Now we can enjoy fresh produce in all seasons and have a number of ways to heat and prepare our food. Life is delicious.

Seasonal Favorites is a celebration of food, the decoration and presentation of that food, and the special days we set aside for feasts. It is full of the tips that most aid us in providing our own bounty and enjoyment. We invite you to literally dig in with The Garden Club of Houston as our members and friends share their family traditions, knowledge and joy—in gardening, floral design, cooking and decoration for special events during the year.

As Auntie Mame said, "Life is a buffet and some poor souls are starving to death. Live, live, live!" Her *joie de vivre* was not directed toward culinary pursuits, but her point is well taken—eat well and live, live, live! Make every calorie delicious and special; it does not have to be expensive. Homemade is best.

Here are our seasonal favorites for you to use for many seasons to come.

Enjoy!

fabulous fall

fabulous *fall*

Labor Day somehow starts the year: It's back to school, back to volunteer work and back to football season, which creates a huge number of social opportunities here in Texas. As we put our white shoes away until next Easter, we begin looking forward to The Garden Club of Houston's Annual Bulb and Plant Mart in early October, and it reminds us of our fall gardening tasks.

We begin our fall planting for spring flowers, and we improve drainage and prepare our flower beds to plant spring-flowering plants, fall-blooming perennials and cold-loving vegetables. We begin raking (never blowing, of course) leaves into the compost pile or onto flower beds, and we search for berries, fall colored leaves, bare branches and pinecones to decorate our homes. We also discover wonderful dried plant material for seasonal ornaments.

In October and November, the bulbs we plant are amaryllis, daffodils, tulips, anemones and hyacinths. Actually, October is the best month to plant everything—including citrus and fruit trees! This is the time to sow seeds for cold-weather vegetables and wildflowers, too. In November, we bring in the tender plants. November also finds us setting out cold-weather plants, our snapdragons, rocket plant (arugula), lettuce, columbine, kale and chard (ornamentals will go through the winter). If slugs find their way to our gardens, we use fennel and rosemary to repel them, or a plate of beer drowns them without sorrows!

Gourds, pumpkins and Indian corn appear at local growers; decorative acorns materialize on branches and the ground. To prepare our gardens for winter rest, we begin to water them less, but we are careful to lavish water on our new plantings to give them a good start. Early

Fall brings so many opportunities to celebrate with our families, friends and colleagues.

on in the fall, we do our last pruning. An unexpected cold snap could kill off new growth.

Fall is a wonderful time to support our local growers, especially at the farmers markets. Local and seasonal produce includes: apples, beets (Nov.), bell peppers, broccoli (Oct.), cantaloupe, carrots, celery, cucumbers, greens, herbs, honeydew, mushrooms, onions, oranges (Oct.), peaches (Oct.), potatoes, squash, sweet potatoes, turnips and watermelon. (Yes, watermelons seem like summer, but they are fresh and yummy.) Best of all, the fall pecan crop is ready! Pumpkins, gourds, rich gold, burnt orange and velvety brown leaf colors festoon our homes, and spices such as ginger, cinnamon and cloves flavor our kitchens.

Fall brings so many opportunities to celebrate with our families, friends and colleagues. From the Labor Day picnic that sends summer finally packing to a tasty Back-to-School brown bag, Columbus Day celebrations, the amazing array of food that appears at the Bulb Mart and the rousing fun of Tailgate parties. Halloween—sometimes hot and sometimes bitter cold here—is always a surprise…and then there's spirited Day of the Dead festivities, Veterans Day, Hunting Season, a warming Harvest Supper and Thanksgiving in all its delicious glory.

We have recipes, party ideas and ways to make your fall even more memorable. We've even included Black Friday, that après-Thanksgiving shopping day, to round out the seasonal activities. And lest we forget the faithful, you'll find a recipe for dog biscuits, too, for observing St. Francis Day or to treat your pooch at any time during the year.

LABOR DAY

For Labor Day, a picnic is in order—barbecue sauces for cooking outside on the grill, plus veggies for the grill, a cool salad and fresh blueberries!

white barbecue sauce

LAURIE LIEDTKE

1-1/2 cups mayonnaise
1/2 cup white wine vinegar
1 tablespoon coarsely ground pepper
1 tablespoon Creole mustard
2 teaspoons prepared horseradish
2 cloves garlic, minced
1 teaspoon salt
1 teaspoon sugar

Whisk together all ingredients until blended.
If you prefer a thinner sauce, add up to
1/4 cup of water. Good with all meats.

MAKES 2 CUPS

gladys' bbq sauce

LAURIE LIEDTKE

2 cups water
I cup vinegar
I cup ketchup
I/2 cup chili sauce
I medium onion, finely grated
2 tablespoons Worcestershire sauce
2 tablespoons brown sugar
I tablespoon Liquid Smoke
I teaspoon garlic powder
I teaspoon salt
I teaspoon pepper
I teaspoon chili powder
I teaspoon Ac'cent, optional
Dash of paprika

In a large saucepan, combine all ingredients. Simmer for 45 minutes. Good on red meats.

MAKES ABOUT 5 CUPS

baby back ribs with espresso barbecue sauce

MARGARET PIERCE

2 racks baby back ribs (4 to 6
   ribs per person)
Grey salt
Freshly ground pepper

sauce:

I/4 cup olive oil
I/4 cup mashed and minced garlic*
2 cups ketchup
2 cups honey
I cup cider vinegar
I/2 cup soy sauce
Pinch of grey salt
2 demitasse cups espresso *or* I/2 cup strong
   coffee *or* instant espresso
Freshly ground pepper to taste

Preheat oven to 325°. Cut each rack of ribs in half along the bone so they can be easily stacked. Rub salt and pepper onto both sides of meat (use salt and pepper liberally because some will inevitably come off in the pan). Stack ribs close together, about three layers high, on a foil-lined baking sheet. Bake for 2 hours, shifting the bottom layer of ribs to the top every 30 minutes, or until the meat is tender and almost falling off the bone.

While the ribs are baking, make the sauce: Add oil to a preheated sauté pan. Sauté garlic until light brown, about 1 minute. Add the ketchup, honey, vinegar and soy sauce; stir well. Add salt, then whisk in coffee. Season with pepper. Simmer for 10 minutes. Cool. The sauce can be made ahead and stored in the refrigerator for up to 2 weeks.

A half hour before serving, transfer ribs to a preheated grill (if using coals, make sure they have burnt down to an ember). Brush ribs with sauce and close grill. Turn ribs and brush with sauce every 10 minutes.

Mash garlic with the side of a knife and then finely mince to release oils.

MAKES 5-6 CUPS SAUCE

Wine Recommendation: Zinfandel, Australian Shiraz or Argentinean Malbec

rosemary biscuit sticks

ROSEMARY FARNASE

3 cups buttermilk biscuit mix
1 tablespoon minced fresh rosemary *or*
   1 teaspoon dried rosemary, crushed
1 cup milk
2 tablespoons olive oil

Preheat oven to 450°. In a large bowl, stir biscuit mix, rosemary and milk to make a soft dough. Turn onto a surface dusted with additional biscuit mix; knead 10 times. Divide dough into 16 pieces. Using the palms of your hands, roll out dough to make long narrow sticks (about 6 inches). Place on a lightly greased baking sheet. Bake for 12-14 minutes or until golden brown.

MAKES 16

terre's california broccoli salad

DANA PARKEY

2 pounds fresh broccoli, cut into
   bite-size pieces
1/2 cup raisins
1/3 cup chopped onion
1-1/2 cups mayonnaise
1/4 cup sugar
3 tablespoons cider vinegar
Freshly ground pepper
6 to 8 bacon strips, cooked and crumbled
1/2 cup sunflower seeds

In a large bowl, toss the broccoli, raisins and onion. In a small bowl, whisk the mayonnaise, sugar, vinegar and pepper. Pour over broccoli mixture and toss to coat. Cover and refrigerate for at least 2 hours. Just before serving, stir in bacon and sunflower seeds.

SERVES 8-10

throw-'em-on-the-grill veggie packets

GAIL ANDERSON

You can assemble these at home and take on a cookout.

4 baby carrots
2 plum tomatoes, quartered lengthwise
2 thick slices eggplant
1 portobello mushroom cap, sliced
1 yellow bell pepper, cut into strips
1 small zucchini, sliced
1 small red onion, cut into strips
1/4 cup prepared vinaigrette *or* Jane's
   Vinaigrette (recipe on page 149)
Salt and pepper to taste

Divide the vegetables evenly between two sheets of heavy-duty foil, piling them in the center. Drizzle each pile with 2 tablespoons vinaigrette. Season with salt and pepper. Fold edges of foil in and wrap tightly, forming two sealed packets. Grill immediately or refrigerate until ready to cook. Place packets on the rack of a medium-hot grill. Cook for 10-15 minutes or until vegetables are sizzling and fragrant. Be careful when opening the foil—the veggies will be steaming!

SERVES 2

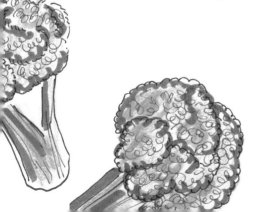

perfectly good
blueberries

KAREN TERRELL

I cup water
3/4 cup sugar
15 juniper berries, crushed
I sprig fresh rosemary (4 inches)
Pinch of salt
2 pints fresh blueberries
I/4 cup dry gin

In a small saucepan, combine the water,
sugar, juniper berries, rosemary and salt.
Bring to a boil; cook and stir for 10-12
minutes or until sugar is dissolved and syrup
is reduced to about 3/4 cup. Place blueberries in a bowl; strain syrup over berries.
Stir in gin. Let stand until cool, about
30 minutes. Serve over vanilla ice cream;
garnish with mint sprigs.

SERVES 12

*Variation: Serve over watermelon; dollop with whipped
topping and garnish with mint.*

very best
blueberry cobbler

MARGARET PIERCE

2-1/2 cups fresh *or* frozen blueberries
Juice of 1/2 lemon
1 teaspoon vanilla extract
1 cup sugar
1/2 teaspoon all-purpose flour
1 tablespoon butter, melted

topping:

1-3/4 cups all-purpose flour
6 tablespoons plus 2 teaspoons sugar, *divided*
4 teaspoons baking powder
5 tablespoons cold butter
1 cup milk (room temperature)
Pinch of ground cinnamon

Preheat oven to 375°. Place blueberries in a lightly greased 8-inch square baking dish; sprinkle with lemon juice and vanilla. Sprinkle with sugar and flour. Stir in melted butter; set aside.

In a bowl, combine the flour, 6 tablespoons sugar and baking powder. Rub in butter using your fingers, or cut in with a pastry blender until it is in small pieces. Make a well in the center and quickly stir in the milk; mix just until moistened. (You should have a very thick batter or very wet dough. You may need to add a splash more milk.) Cover and let rest for 10 minutes.

Spoon batter over blueberries, leaving only a few small holes for the berries to peek through. Add cinnamon to the remaining sugar; sprinkle over batter. Bake for 20-25 minutes or until golden brown and a knife inserted into the topping comes out clean. Let cool until just warm before serving. This can be refrigerated for 2 days. Serve with vanilla ice cream.

SERVES 6

BACK TO SCHOOL

For healthy snacks, try adding sliced fruit to sandwiches, and include home-baked
breads and cookies. New technology in lunch "pails" allows for dips or guacamole
to remain cool, so send along veggies for dipping.

apple bread

DOROTHEA FAUBION

2 cups diced peeled McIntosh apples
I cup sugar
I teaspoon ground cinnamon
I egg, lightly beaten
I/2 cup canola oil
I-I/2 cups all-purpose flour
I teaspoon baking soda
I/8 teaspoon salt
I cup chopped pecans

Preheat oven to 350°. In a bowl, toss the apples with sugar and cinnamon. Stir in egg and oil. Sift the flour with baking soda and salt; stir into apple mixture just until moistened. Fold in pecans. Pour into a greased loaf pan. Bake for I hour or until a toothpick comes out clean.

MAKES I LOAF

chocolate crackle cookies

MARGARET PIERCE

1 package (19.8 ounces) fudge brownie mix
1 cup all-purpose flour
1 egg
1/2 cup water
1/4 cup vegetable oil
1 cup (6 ounces) semisweet chocolate chips
Powdered sugar

Preheat oven to 350°. In a mixing bowl, combine the brownie mix, flour, egg, water and oil; mix well. Stir in chocolate chips. Pour powdered sugar into a shallow bowl. Drop dough by tablespoonfuls into sugar and roll to coat. Place 2 inches apart on greased baking sheets. Bake for 8-10 minutes or until set (don't overbake—cookies will firm up once set). Remove to wire racks to cool.

MAKES 2 DOZEN

ginny pierce's scotcharoos

MARGARET PIERCE

1 cup sugar
1 cup corn syrup
1 cup peanut butter
6 cups crisp rice cereal
1 package (12 ounces) semisweet
   chocolate chips
1 package (10 to 11 ounces) butterscotch chips

In a large saucepan, bring sugar and corn syrup to a boil. Remove from the heat; stir in peanut butter. Gradually stir in cereal and mix well. Transfer to a lightly buttered 13-inch x 9-inch x 2-inch pan; cool. Melt chocolate and butterscotch chips together; spread over bars. Let stand until set. Cut into 1-inch squares.

MAKES 4 DOZEN

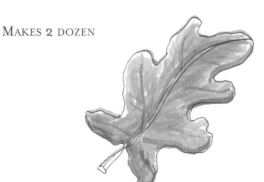

neiman marcus chocolate chip cookies

The popular recipe for these cookies—named because they are so rich—has been circulating from recipe box to recipe box for years. It makes such a large batch that it will feed the entire PTA!

2 cups butter, softened

2 cups sugar

2 cups packed brown sugar

4 eggs, lightly beaten

2 teaspoons vanilla extract

5 cups oatmeal powder*

4 cups all-purpose flour

2 teaspoons baking powder

2 teaspoons baking soda

1 teaspoon salt

1 package (24 ounces) semisweet
   chocolate chips

2 large milk chocolate candy bars (4.4
   ounces *each*)**, grated

3 cups chopped nuts

Preheat oven to 375°. With a mixer, cream butter and sugars. Beat in eggs and vanilla. Combine the oat powder, flour, baking powder, baking soda and salt; gradually add to creamed mixture and mix well. Fold in chocolate chips, candy bar and nuts. Roll into balls. Place 2 inches apart on cookie sheets. Bake for 10 minutes.

* Blend old-fashioned oats in a blender to a fine powder to measure 5 cups.

** You need 8 ounces of grated chocolate bar for the cookies, so keep a little out to nibble on while baking!

MAKES ABOUT 9 DOZEN

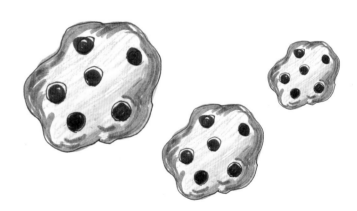

grammie's brownies

MARGARET PIERCE

1/2 cup butter, softened
1 cup sugar
4 eggs, beaten
1 can (16 ounces) chocolate syrup
1 cup all-purpose flour
Pinch of salt
Chopped nuts, optional

chocolate icing:

6 tablespoons butter
1-1/3 to 1-1/2 cups sugar
6 tablespoons milk
1/3 to 1/2 cup semisweet chocolate chips

Preheat oven to 350°. With a mixer, cream butter and sugar. Adding one ingredient at a time, beat in eggs, chocolate syrup, flour and salt. Fold in nuts if you like. Pour into a greased and floured 15-inch x 10-inch x 1-inch baking pan. Bake for 30 minutes. Cool.

To make icing: In a small saucepan, bring the butter, sugar and milk to a boil. Remove from the heat; stir in chips until icing reaches desired spreading consistency. Immediately spread over brownies.

MAKES 2-1/2 DOZEN

school lunch box ideas

- Cut bread for sandwiches with a star, heart or other favorite shapes of cookie cutters.
- Use a hot dog bun instead of bread for a change.
- Add fruit to sandwiches—apple slices on peanut butter 'n' jelly...pear slices on turkey...orange or pineapple on ham.
- Toast pecans or walnuts to add crunch to chicken and tuna salad sandwiches.
- Spread a layer of cranberry sauce on a turkey or chicken sandwich.
- Take a taco! Stuff a tortilla with shredded chicken, cheese and lettuce and include mild taco sauce.
- Make pinwheels—flatten soft bread with a rolling pin; spread with peanut butter and jelly. Roll up, wrap in plastic wrap and refrigerate overnight. The next morning, slice and secure with pretty toothpicks.
- Send fruit salad with a container of vanilla yogurt.
- Mix fruit salad into a container of cottage cheese.
- Combine cream cheese softened with milk and a few drops of Worcestershire sauce— it's a tasty dip for carrots and celery sticks or pretzels.
- Pack guacamole and chips—it'll make their day!

more school lunch box ideas

Old Waldorf Salad: chopped apple, orange, celery, walnuts or sunflower seeds and raisins, with a slice of ham or chicken and pita bread.

Fruity Cottage Cheese Salad: peaches and sunflower seeds in cottage cheese.

Pita Pocket Salad Sandwich: grated carrot, chopped celery and red pepper, lettuce and tomatoes in pita bread.

Rabbit Salad: cottage cheese with chopped raisins, chopped carrots and lettuce or cabbage, halved grapes, nuts of choice.

Apple Sandwich: cut an apple in half and hollow out the core; fill with Rabbit Salad.

Apple Krispies: gently mix peanut butter and Rice Krispies; press on apple cubes.

COLUMBUS DAY

All Italians know that Columbus was an Italian, even though he discovered the New World under the flag of Spain. Here are some Italian-inspired recipes to serve around the second Monday in October...or anytime.

bruschetta al arugula

MIMI KERR

2 handfuls arugula leaves
2 slices country-style bread
1 clove garlic, lightly crushed
2 tablespoons grated *or* shaved
   Parmesan cheese
Salt and freshly ground pepper to taste
1 to 2 tablespoons olive oil

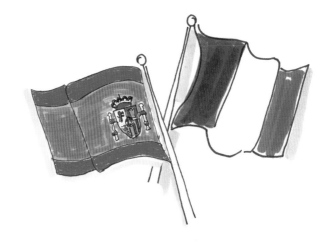

Roll arugula in bundles and slice crosswise into strips. Toast bread on a grill or in the toaster; while it's still hot, rub one side of the toast with garlic. Top with arugula, Parmesan, salt and pepper. Pour a thin stream of oil over the top.

SERVES 2

caponata siciliana

MARY TRAINER

2/3 cup olive oil, *divided*
2 medium onions, finely diced
I cup diced celery
I can (28 ounces) whole tomatoes in juice
1/3 cup red *or* white wine vinegar
6 tablespoons sugar
2 teaspoons salt
1/4 teaspoon pepper
Cayenne pepper to taste
I teaspoon Italian seasoning
I large eggplant, cut into 1/2-inch cubes
I can (4.5 ounces) sliced ripe olives
2 teaspoons capers with some juice
2 teaspoons pine nuts

Heat 1/3 cup oil in a large skillet; add onions
and remaining oil. Cook until onions are
translucent. Add celery and tomatoes. Cook
over medium heat for 15 minutes or until
sauce thickens. Stir in the vinegar, sugar,
salt, pepper, cayenne and Italian seasoning.
Add eggplant. Cover and cook for 10 minutes. Add olives, capers and pine nuts. Cook,
uncovered, for 10 minutes. Taste and add
more vinegar if a sharper flavor is desired.
Serve at room temperature as a side dish
or relish.

southern italian calamari pasta

GAIL HENDRYX

Briny and piquant, this seems like a perfect seaside dish. It is less a pasta dish than a dish with some pasta in it. It is also easy for company, since you can cook the sauce ahead of time and just add the pasta and calamari when you are ready to dine. I like to use whole-wheat pasta and serve this with broiled asparagus plus spinach salad with strawberries and toasted sesame seeds.

1/2 pound rotini pasta
Olive oil
1/4 cup pine nuts *or* sliced almonds
5 cloves garlic, finely chopped
3 tablespoons capers, rinsed
2 tablespoons currants
2 tablespoons dried cranberries
1 tablespoon red pepper flakes
   (or less if you are squeamish)
2 cups good tomato sauce (see Nora's
   Tomato Sauce on page 202)
1 cup white wine
3 to 4 sprigs fresh thyme
1-1/2 pounds calamari, cleaned and sliced
   into 1/3-inch rounds
6 scallions, sliced
Kosher salt and freshly ground
   pepper to taste

Boil the pasta in salted water until it is about a minute underdone. Drain and save the water; set pasta aside. Cover the bottom of a large sauté pan with a thin layer of oil; heat. Add nuts, garlic, capers, currants, cranberries and pepper flakes; sauté enough to toast the nuts, but don't go so far as to burn the garlic. Add the tomato sauce, wine and thyme; simmer for 5-10 minutes or until flavors are blended.

Add the pasta; simmer a few more minutes. If too thick, add some reserved pasta cooking water or more wine. As the pasta finishes cooking, add the calamari. It is finished when the calamari turns opaque, which will only take a couple of minutes (don't cook longer or it will be tough). Stir in the scallions. Season as needed with salt and pepper (this dish is relatively salty, so more salt will probably not be needed). Serve with additional scallions and olive oil on top if desired.

SERVES 4

*Wine Recommendation: a crisp dry white such as
Haak Vineyards Blanc du Bois*

jennifer's chicken tetrazzini

DANA PARKEY

1 package (16 ounces) vermicelli
4 cups cubed cooked chicken
1 package (10 ounces) frozen Welsh rarebit*
2 cans (10.75 ounces *each*) condensed
   cream of mushroom soup
2 cups chicken broth
1/4 cup sherry *or* Marsala
2 to 3 cans (4 ounces *each*) sliced
   mushrooms, drained *or* 8 ounces sliced
   fresh mushrooms
1 bunch parsley, chopped
1/2 cup grated Parmesan cheese
Paprika

Preheat oven to 325°. Cook vermicelli as the box directs. Meanwhile, in a large pot, combine the chicken, rarebit, soup, broth, sherry and mushrooms; cook and stir until cheese is melted, adding more broth if needed. Drain vermicelli; add to the chicken mixture. Spoon into a greased 13-inch x 9-inch x 2-inch baking dish. Sprinkle with parsley, Parmesan and paprika. Cover and bake for 45 minutes. Uncover; bake 5-15 minutes longer or until bubbly and heated through.

* Look for Stouffer's Welsh Rarebit in the freezer section of your grocery store; you may want to call the store ahead to see if they carry it or can order it for you.

SERVES 6-8

Wine Recommendation: for white, Chardonnay, Viognier or Alsace Riesling...for red, Côtes du Rhône, Merlot or Sangiovese

grilled italian sausage with fresh vegetables and herbs

NORA WATSON

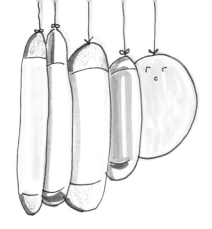

This dish can be prepared ahead of time—after grilling the sausages and vegetables, layer in a casserole and then heat when you're ready to eat. Serve with warm crusty bread...and don't forget the salad and wine!

Green and red bell peppers, onions and
    tomatoes, sliced lengthwise (*plan on a*
    quarter to a half of each vegetable per person)
Chopped fresh parsley, thyme, basil
    and oregano
Unpeeled whole garlic cloves
Olive oil
Salt and pepper
Mild *or* hot Italian sausages (*1 to 2 per person*)

Preheat the grill. Place vegetables, herbs and garlic on a large sheet of heavy-duty foil (may need to assemble several packets, depending on how many vegetables you are making). Drizzle with oil; sprinkle with salt and pepper. Fold foil over; crimp and seal tightly. Grill sausages until done—a little crisp on the outside. Grill vegetable packet for 20 minutes, turning once (vegetables should sizzle inside).

Open foil carefully to allow steam to escape; squeeze softened garlic over vegetables. Transfer to a serving dish; serve with sausages. If making ahead, empty grilled vegetable packet into a deep casserole dish; layer grilled sausages on top and cover with foil. Refrigerate. Before serving, place casserole in a 350° oven long enough to heat through.

Wine Recommendation: Zinfandel, American Cabernet, Australian Shiraz or Argentinean Malbec

italian pot roast

MARGARET GRIFFITH

1 boneless beef chuck *or* rump
   roast (3 pounds)
3 large cloves garlic, cut into slivers
1/4 cup olive oil, *divided*
1 pound onions, chopped
2 carrots, chopped
2 ribs celery, chopped
1/2 cup dry red wine
1 cup chopped seeded plum tomatoes
1 tablespoon tomato paste
1/4 cup finely chopped fresh basil
Salt and freshly ground pepper to taste

With the point of a sharp knife, pierce roast
in several places; insert garlic slivers into
holes. Heat 2 tablespoons oil in a heavy 3- or
4-quart casserole or Dutch oven. Brown the
roast on all sides over medium heat; remove.
Add remaining oil to the pan; sauté onions,
carrots and celery until moderately browned.
Stir in wine. Cook for 2-3 minutes, scraping
browned bits from pan bottom. Add tomatoes, tomato paste, basil, salt and pepper.
Return roast to the pan; cover tightly. Cook
over very low heat for 3 hours, turning
occasionally, or until meat is very tender.

Remove roast and keep warm. If serving
immediately, skim fat from cooking juices;
purée in a food processor and reheat. If
making ahead, refrigerate the meat and
juices overnight. Remove any congealed fat
from the cooking juices; purée in a food
processor. Reheat the meat in the juices
before serving.

SERVES 6-8

Wine Recommendation: same wine used to braise the beef,
or Merlot, Shiraz or Châteauneuf-du-Pape

pasta with chicken, mushrooms and arugula

ROSEMARY DIGIORNNO

6 ounces fresh mushrooms
3 cloves garlic
1/4 cup olive oil
1-1/4 pounds boneless skinless chicken
   thighs, cut into 1/2-inch pieces
   (ask butcher!)
Salt and pepper for seasoning chicken
1 small onion, chopped
3/4 teaspoon chopped fresh rosemary
1/2 teaspoon salt

1/4 teaspoon pepper
3 tablespoons balsamic vinegar
1 can (28 ounces) whole tomatoes in juice
1/2 pound penne pasta
5 ounces baby arugula (about 8 cups)

In a food processor, finely chop mushrooms and garlic; set aside. Heat oil in an iron skillet over medium-high heat until hot. Season chicken with salt and pepper; sauté in oil in batches until browned, about 6 minutes. Remove chicken. Reduce heat to medium and sauté onion until softened, about 3 minutes. Add mushroom mixture, rosemary, salt and pepper. Cook, stirring constantly, until mixture begins to brown, about 4 minutes. Add vinegar and cook until evaporated.

Cook pasta until al dente. Meanwhile, add chicken and tomatoes to mushroom mixture. Simmer, breaking up tomatoes with a spoon and stirring occasionally, until sauce thickens, about 15 minutes. Reduce heat to very low; stir in arugula. Cover until wilted. Drain pasta and stir into chicken mixture; cook for 1 minute.

SERVES 4

Wine Recommendation: Chianti Classico, Pinot Noir or Côtes du Rhône

patate con due formaggi

DODIE JACKSON

3 tablespoons butter
3 tablespoons all-purpose flour
3 cups milk
4 large baking potatoes, peeled and thinly sliced
1 large yellow onion, sliced into thin rounds
4 cloves garlic, mashed
2 cups grated Romano cheese
Dash of kosher salt
1 tablespoon pepper
1 cup grated Parmesan cheese

Preheat oven to 350°. In a saucepan over medium heat, melt butter; add flour and stir for 1 minute. Slowly add milk, stirring until mixture is smooth, not lumpy. Bring to a slight boil and remove from the heat. In a large greased baking dish, layer potatoes, onion, garlic and Romano. Pour white sauce over the top; sprinkle with salt, pepper and Parmesan. Bake, uncovered, for 1 hour or until browned.

SERVES 8

white beans with olive oil, tomatoes and sage

MARGARET GRIFFITH

1 pound dried Great Northern *or*
   other white beans
1 bunch fresh sage
6 cloves garlic
1/2 cup olive oil
1/4 cup coarsely chopped fresh sage
2 tablespoons coarsely chopped garlic
8 medium tomatoes (about 2 pounds),
   peeled and coarsely chopped
Salt and pepper to taste

Place beans in a large heavy saucepan. Add enough water to cover by 3 inches. Add the bunch of sage and whole garlic cloves. Soak overnight. Bring beans to a boil in soaking liquid. Reduce heat; cover and simmer until tender, about 1 hour. Drain; discard sage and garlic. Can be prepared 1 day ahead. Cover and refrigerate.

Heat oil in a large heavy saucepan over medium heat. Sauté chopped sage and garlic until garlic is golden, about 2 minutes. Add tomatoes; cook until sauce thickens slightly, about 10 minutes. Add beans. Season with salt and pepper. Cook until heated through, about 5 minutes. Good served at room temperature.

SERVES 6-8

italian strawberries

GAIL HENDRYX

Popular in the times of the Roman Empire, strawberries in balsamic vinegar were served over ice brought down from the Alps. This dish continues to delight.

1 pound fresh strawberries
1/4 cup balsamic vinegar
2 tablespoons sugar
1/4 teaspoon pepper

Wash and cut strawberries into halves and quarters and place in a bowl. Combine the vinegar, sugar and pepper; pour over berries. Refrigerate for several hours or overnight. Serve over ice cream or pound cake or both!

SERVES 4

osso buco

This traditional veal dish can be prepared the night before. After baking, you may choose to strain the sauce, pressing hard on the vegetables before discarding. This way, when you take it out of the refrigerator, you can skim the fat before heating it up for dinner.

1/4 cup butter
1-1/2 cups finely chopped onions
1/2 cup finely chopped carrots
1/2 cup finely chopped celery
1 teaspoon finely chopped garlic (or more)
6 to 7 pounds veal shank, cut into 8 pieces*
Salt and freshly ground pepper
All-purpose flour
6 to 8 tablespoons olive oil, *divided*
1 cup dry white wine
3 cups drained canned whole tomatoes,
   coarsely chopped
3/4 cup beef *or* chicken stock
6 parsley sprigs
2 bay leaves
1/2 teaspoon dried basil
1/2 teaspoon dried thyme

gremolata:

3 tablespoons finely chopped parsley
1 tablespoon grated lemon peel
1 teaspoon finely chopped garlic

Under the Tuscan Sun Dinner ~ Karen Terrell

For a birthday, anniversary or other special autumn occasion, why not try this hearty Italian menu? It will bring a bit of sunshine to any celebration! The Osso Buco and Risotto with Saffron and Parmesan take a little more time to make, but the effort is well worth it. For dessert, I suggest a Classic Italian Cream Cake. For an appetizer, you might serve Bruschetta al Arugula (page 23)...and for a salad, one of Paule's Farmers Market Salads (page 38).

Choose a heavy shallow casserole or Dutch oven that has a tight cover and is just large enough to snugly hold pieces of veal standing up in one layer. Melt butter in the casserole over medium heat; when foam subsides, add onions, carrots, celery and garlic. Cook, stirring occasionally, for 10-15 minutes or until vegetables are lightly colored. Remove from the heat.

Season veal with salt and pepper; roll in flour and shake off excess. In a large heavy skillet, heat 6 tablespoons oil until a haze forms over it. Brown veal over medium-high heat, four pieces at a time, adding more oil if needed. Stand veal pieces up side by side on top of vegetables in baking dish.

Preheat oven to 350°. Leaving just a film of fat in the skillet, add the wine and boil briskly until reduced to about 1/2 cup. Scrape any browned bits clinging to the pan. Stir in tomatoes, stock, parsley, bay leaves, basil and thyme. Bring to a boil, then pour over the veal. (The liquid should come halfway up the side of the veal; if it doesn't, add more stock.) Bring the casserole to a boil on top of the stove. Cover and bake in the lower third of the oven, basting occasionally and regulating oven heat to keep the casserole simmering gently. In about 1-1/4 hours, the

veal should be tender; test it by piercing the meat with the tip of a sharp knife.

Combine the gremolata ingredients. To serve, arrange veal pieces on a heated platter; spoon vegetables and sauce from the casserole around them. Sprinkle gremolata on top. Serve additional sauce in a gravy boat and additional gremolata in a dish to pass.

Veal pieces should be 2-1/2 inches long and tied around their circumference with string (ask the butcher!).

SERVES 6-8

risotto with saffron and parmesan

7 cups chicken stock
1/2 cup butter, softened, *divided*
1/2 cup chopped onion
1/3 to 1/2 cup chopped uncooked beef
   marrow, optional*
2 cups uncooked Arborio rice
1/2 cup dry white wine
1/8 teaspoon saffron threads, crushed
   to a powder
1/2 cup freshly grated Parmesan cheese

Bring stock to a simmer in a large saucepan; keep it barely simmering over low heat. In a heavy 3-quart saucepan, melt 1/4 cup butter over medium heat. Sauté onion for 7-8 minutes (do not brown). Stir in marrow if desired. Add rice; cook and stir for 1-2 minutes or until grains glisten with butter and are somewhat opaque. Add wine; boil until almost completely absorbed. Add 2 cups simmering stock; cook, uncovered, stirring occasionally, until almost all of the liquid is absorbed.

Add 2 more cups of stock and continue to cook, stirring occasionally. Meanwhile, stir the saffron into 2 cups stock and let it steep for a few minutes, then pour over the rice. Cook until stock is completely absorbed. By now the rice should be tender. If it is still firm, add the remaining stock, 1/2 cup at a time. Continue cooking and stirring until rice is soft. With a fork, gently stir in the Parmesan and remaining butter. Serve at once while rice is creamy and piping hot.

* If you want to use the marrow in this recipe, just ask your butcher for an extra marrowbone.

SERVES 6-8

*Wine Recommendation: for white, Soave or Gavi...
for red, Chianti Classico*

classic italian cream cake

For decoration, top off the cake with a few perfect pecan halves in the shape of a sun or flower. You can make this cake a day ahead, or even two, if you store it in a tight container.

1 teaspoon baking soda
1 cup buttermilk
1/2 cup butter
1/2 cup shortening
2 cups sugar
5 eggs, *separated*
2 cups sifted all-purpose flour
1 teaspoon vanilla extract
1 cup chopped pecans
1-1/3 cups flaked coconut*

cream cheese frosting:

1 package (8 ounces) cream cheese, softened
1/2 cup butter, softened
1 teaspoon vanilla extract
1 box (1 pound) powdered sugar

Preheat oven to 325°. Have all ingredients at room temperature. Add baking soda to buttermilk; let stand for a few minutes. With a mixer, cream butter and shortening with sugar for 3-5 minutes until light and fluffy.

Add egg yolks, one at a time, beating well after each addition. Add buttermilk alternately with flour. Stir in vanilla. Beat egg whites until stiff; fold into batter. Gently fold in pecans and coconut. Divide among three greased and floured 9-inch cake pans (line pans with waxed paper if desired). Bake for 25 minutes or until a toothpick comes out clean. Cool for 10 minutes; remove from pans to wire racks to cool completely.

To make frosting: With a mixer, beat cream cheese and butter until well blended. Beat in vanilla. Gradually beat in powdered sugar, a little at a time, until frosting is smooth and reaches spreading consistency. Spread between layers and over top and sides of cake.

* You may use freshly grated coconut if you like, and toast half of it to light golden brown.

SERVES 12

Wine Recommendation: Vin Santo, Prosecco or an Asti

ST. FRANCIS DAY

*St. Francis loved animals, and many churches bless
the animals in early October.*

barley beef dog biscuits

MEG TAPP

*These dog treats are quite edible for humans; however,
getting them to the desired crunchiness for no crumbs on
the carpet—and to keep canine teeth sharp and clean—
means leaving them in the oven overnight. They make
the kitchen smell good, too. Not human tested. No
animals were harmed in the development of this recipe.
Bone appétit!*

1/2 cup olive oil
1/4 cup dried parsley flakes
2 cups beef broth
2 cups barley flour
3 to 4 cups rye flour

Preheat oven to 350°. In a large mixing
bowl, combine oil and parsley. Heat broth
until steaming; pour into mixing bowl.
Mix in barley flour. Cool until lukewarm.
Gradually blend in rye flour until dough is
stiff. Using dough hook, mix for 3 minutes
or until dough is smooth.

Roll teaspoonfuls of dough into balls. Mash
into disk shapes and place on an ungreased
cookie sheet. (These biscuits will not spread,
so not much space is needed between them.)
Bake for 30 minutes. Remove from oven
and turn over. Reduce heat to 325°. Bake
30 minutes longer. Turn oven off and let
biscuits cool completely. Overnight is ideal.
Store at room temperature.

MAKES ABOUT 50 SILVER-DOLLAR-SIZE TREATS

BULB AND PLANT MART

*Following in the footsteps of our first cookbook—"Perennial Favorites"—we
present more recipes from the covered-dish banquet that is the volunteer workers'
hospitality room. Weary from bagging bulbs and tagging potted plants, the workers
can relax and regain strength with food that is eagerly anticipated each year.
Weight is invariably gained during the sale, even with the heavy lifting.*

lollie's blueberry cream muffins

LOLLIE CLUETT

Keep these in the freezer and enjoy for breakfast.

2 eggs
I cup sugar
I/2 cup vegetable oil
I/2 teaspoon vanilla extract
2 cups all-purpose flour
I/2 teaspoon baking soda
I/2 teaspoon salt
I cup (8 ounces) sour cream
I cup fresh *or* frozen blueberries

Preheat oven to 400°. In a mixing bowl,
beat eggs. Gradually add sugar. Continue
beating while slowly adding oil. Add vanilla.
Combine the flour, baking soda and salt;
add to egg mixture alternately with sour
cream. Fold in blueberries (do not thaw if
using frozen berries). Spoon into greased
muffin cups. Bake for 20 minutes or until
a toothpick comes out clean.

MAKES I-I/2 DOZEN

*Variation: For fruitier muffins, decrease the sugar to
3/4 cup and use 1-1/2 cups of blueberries.*

basil pesto torta

BETTY DAVIS

Absolutely elegant for cocktail parties!

pesto:

4 cups fresh basil
1/2 cup flat-leaf parsley
1/3 cup pine nuts, lightly toasted
4 cloves garlic
2 teaspoons pepper
1-1/2 teaspoons salt
3/4 cup olive oil
3/4 cup grated Parmesan cheese

spread:

2 packages (8 ounces *each*) cream
  cheese, softened
1/2 cup sour cream
Juice of 1 lemon
1 bunch green onions, chopped
1 cup pine nuts
1 cup dried cranberries
1 cup pesto

To make pesto: Place the basil, parsley, nuts, garlic, pepper and salt in a food processor; pulse until herbs and nuts are finely chopped. While processor is running, add oil in a thin steady stream. Add Parmesan; pulse until blended. Set 1 cup aside for spread; refrigerate or freeze remaining pesto for another use.

Line two 3-cup containers with plastic wrap. Blend cream cheese, sour cream and lemon juice. Sprinkle 1/4 cup each of the green onions, pine nuts and cranberries in each container; add 1/4 cup pesto and a layer of cream cheese mixture. Repeat layers. Refrigerate until serving. Unmold torta onto a serving platter; serve with crackers.

SERVES 20

paule's farmers market salads

PAULE JOHNSTON

I'm a big fan of all the local farmers markets and most heartily recommend that you find one in your neighborhood. The beautiful colors and fresh taste of these salads cannot be overemphasized!

paule's vinaigrette:

1 part olive oil to 2 parts vegetable oil (two-thirds of the total amount)
1 part apple cider vinegar to 2 parts lemon juice (for the rest)

Pour into a jar and shake until emulsified. Taste and add what you think it needs of any of the ingredients.

paule's beet salad:

1 pound small farm-market-fresh beets (any color)
Paule's Vinaigrette
Lemon juice, sea salt and freshly ground pepper to taste

Steam beets until tender (al dente); peel off outer skin (it usually sort of slips off). Cut beets into small cubes; toss with vinaigrette several hours before serving. Test for sweetness before serving; add lemon juice, salt and pepper if needed.

paule's fresh kale:

1 pound farm-market-fresh kale
Paule's Vinaigrette plus 1 to 2 teaspoons soy sauce
Sea salt and freshly ground pepper to taste

Remove the spine of the kale; tear kale into small pieces. Toss with vinaigrette and soy sauce 1-2 hours before serving. Season with salt and pepper.

shrimp rice salad

BETH WRAY

For the French dressing, I prefer La Martinique. To simplify, purchase precooked and peeled shrimp, chopped vegetables and sliced olives. This is also good served hot.

I pound shrimp, boiled, peeled and deveined
2 cups cooked rice
I/2 cup thinly sliced celery
I/4 cup chopped green bell pepper
I/4 cup thinly sliced olives
I/4 cup chopped pimientos
I/4 cup chopped onion
I/4 teaspoon freshly ground pepper
I/8 teaspoon garlic salt
I/8 teaspoon celery salt
3 to 4 tablespoons French dressing
Lettuce leaves, tomato wedges and
  celery leaves

In a large bowl, combine the first II ingredients and toss lightly. Refrigerate until chilled. Serve on lettuce, garnished with tomato wedges and celery leaves.

SERVES 4

Wine Recommendation: Sauvignon Blanc or Sancerre

chicken pecan salad with cranberries

MIMI KERR

2 boneless skinless chicken breasts
I cup diced celery
3/4 cup dried cranberries
I egg*
2 tablespoons cider vinegar
I-I/2 tablespoons sugar
I teaspoon Dijon mustard
I/2 teaspoon salt
I/2 cup vegetable oil
I/4 cup olive oil
Pepper and additional salt to taste
I cup coarsely chopped pecans
Lettuce leaves

Poach and shred the chicken; place in a large bowl with celery and cranberries. In a food processor, blend the egg, vinegar, sugar, mustard and salt. While the processor is running, slowly add oil and blend well. Pour over chicken mixture and toss to coat; season with pepper and salt. Cover and refrigerate for several hours. Just before serving, add pecans and toss gently. Serve over lettuce.

SERVES 4

* If you prefer to not use uncooked egg in the dressing, just leave it out; the dressing will be thinner.

cold curried pea soup

DORIS HEARD

5 pounds frozen green peas
9 onions, chopped
9 carrots, chopped
9 ribs celery, chopped
9 potatoes, peeled and diced
6 to 8 cloves garlic, pressed
3 tablespoons curry powder
3 tablespoons salt
4-1/2 quarts chicken broth, *divided*
I quart cream
I quart milk

topping:

I cup (8 ounces) plain low-fat yogurt
1/2 cup chopped fresh cilantro
1/4 cup chopped red onion

In a stockpot, simmer the vegetables and
seasonings in I quart broth until tender.
Purée. Add remaining broth. Refrigerate.
When ready to serve, stir in cream and milk
and adjust seasoning. Serve cold, or reheat
and serve hot. For "silken" soup, strain
purée through wet cheesecloth and sieve.
Combine topping ingredients; add a dollop
to each bowl.

MAKES 5-1/2 GALLONS

cold creamy cucumber soup

LOLLIE CLUETT

Easy and delicious!

4 cucumbers
1-1/2 cups buttermilk
I cup (8 ounces) sour cream
1/4 cup olive oil
2-1/4 teaspoons minced fresh dill *or*
  1/2 teaspoon dill weed
1-1/2 teaspoons salt
I teaspoon white wine vinegar
1/2 teaspoon balsamic vinegar

Peel cucumbers and halve lengthwise; use a
spoon to scrape out the seeds. Coarsely chop
cucumbers; combine with the remaining
ingredients. Purée mixture in a food processor in two batches until smooth. Refrigerate
until chilled.

SERVES 6

deviled eggs

DANA PARKEY

Deviled eggs are the first food to go from the hospitality room table.

6 hard-boiled eggs
1 to 2 tablespoons mayonnaise
1 to 1-1/2 tablespoons pickle relish
1 teaspoon prepared mustard
1/8 teaspoon salt
Dash of pepper
Paprika

Slice eggs in half lengthwise and carefully remove yolks. Mash yolks with mayonnaise. Add relish, mustard, salt and pepper; mix well. Spoon into egg whites. Sprinkle with paprika.

MAKES 1 DOZEN

Variation: Add chopped black olives or diced cocktail onions in place of pickle relish.

Anita Stude's hard-boiled eggs dipped in truffle salt are amazing! Look for truffle salt online at amazon.com or Dean & DeLuca.

mary gray lester's best pimiento cheese

LINDA GRIFFIN

Pimiento cheese is always a favorite!

1 jar (4 ounces) diced pimientos with juice
1 tablespoon diced white onion
1 clove garlic, pressed
1 teaspoon sugar
2 tablespoons mayonnaise
1 tablespoon Durkee's Dressing
Pepper to taste
14 ounces Colby cheese, shredded

In a bowl, mix together the first seven ingredients. Gently blend in cheese.

MAKES ABOUT 1 QUART

cornmeal
sugar cookies

BEV WIEMER

1/2 cup butter, softened
1/3 cup powdered sugar
1 teaspoon lemon zest
1/2 teaspoon vanilla extract
2/3 cup all-purpose flour
1/4 cup cornmeal
2 tablespoons cornstarch
1/4 teaspoon salt
Sugar for sprinkling

In a food processor, blend the butter,
powdered sugar, lemon zest and vanilla.
Add flour, cornmeal, cornstarch and
salt; blend until it comes together. Chill
until easy to handle. Preheat oven to 350°.
On a floured surface, roll out dough to
1/3-inch thickness. Cut out with floured
cookie cutters. Sprinkle with sugar.
Place on greased baking sheets. Bake for
12-14 minutes.

MAKES 2 DOZEN

TAILGATING

Tailgaiting just wouldn't be possible without chili con queso, other dips and chips. The party outside the stadium often is more fun than the football game...unless your team wins.

ann and tom's chili con queso

ANN KELSEY

This recipe was inspired by Jose's Dip—our family's favorite hors d'oeuvre—at Molina's Restaurant on Westheimer Road in Houston. We like to serve this with a big bowl of tortilla chips or fresh tostadas from Molina's or Ninfa's.

1 pound lean ground beef
1 white onion, chopped
3 tablespoons chili powder
2 tablespoons ground cumin
2 pounds Velveeta cheese
1 pound cheddar cheese
2 cans (10 ounces *each*) Ro-Tel tomatoes
2 to 3 jalapeños *or* Serranos, chopped

In a skillet, cook the beef with onion, chili powder and cumin until meat is browned and the flavors are well mixed. While the beef is cooking, slice the cheeses into thick strips; melt in a double boiler or in a pot set in a pan of water. Drain tomatoes, reserving liquid from one can. As the cheese is melting, add the tomatoes and jalapeños. Stir in the meat mixture. Add reserved tomato liquid if you prefer a thinner dip. Taste and adjust the seasoning. Serve warm with tortilla chips or tostadas.

MAKES ABOUT 9 CUPS

guadalajara guacamole

LINDA GRIFFIN

For my guacamole, I blend in just enough homemade pico de gallo to taste, then serve the rest of the pico on the side with fresh chips. Frying your own corn tortillas in a little oil in a skillet is the best…fry just enough to crisp!

1-1/2 pounds plum tomatoes, seeded
  and chopped
3/4 cup chopped white onion
1/2 cup chopped fresh cilantro
3 tablespoons lime *or* lemon juice
3 tablespoons minced seeded jalapeños
Salt and freshly ground pepper to taste
2 ripe avocados

In a bowl, combine the tomatoes, onion, cilantro, lime juice, jalapeños, salt and pepper. In another bowl, mash the avocados with a fork; add tomato mixture, 2 table-spoons at a time, to taste. If you don't add all of the tomato mixture, serve it on the side.

texas tailgate party mix

INGRID KELLY

This goes well with adult beverages before a game. It also makes a very nice Christmas gift; its other name is "Texas Trash," and I gave it for Christmas one year in miniature plastic trash cans.

3 cups Corn Chex
3 cups Rice Chex
3 cups Wheat Chex
1 cup peanuts
1 cup pecan halves
1 cup mini pretzels *or* thin pretzel sticks
6 tablespoons butter
2 tablespoons Worcestershire sauce
1-1/2 teaspoons seasoned salt
3/4 teaspoon garlic powder
Pinch of cayenne pepper

Preheat oven to 250°. Mix the cereals, nuts and pretzels in a large bowl. Place butter in a large roasting pan; place in the oven until melted. Remove pan from oven. Stir in seasonings. Gradually stir in cereal mixture until evenly coated. Bake for 1 hour, stirring every 15 minutes. Spread on paper towels to cool. Store in an airtight container.

SERVES A CROWD OF FANS

"another" pasta salad

LINEY ROTAN

This is really good with brisket and sliced tomatoes.

1 package (16 ounces) macaroni
1 can (15 ounces) green peas, drained
1 cup diced celery
1 cup diced onion
3/4 cup mayonnaise (or more)
1 tablespoon hot Dijon mustard
Salt and freshly ground pepper to taste

Cook macaroni until tender; drain and rinse
in cold water. Place in a large bowl and stir
in the remaining ingredients. Refrigerate
until chilled.

SERVES 10

armstrong ranch curry dressing

SARITA HIXON

*The Armstrong Ranch is a part of Texas history.
Established in 1852, less than 20 years after the Battle of
the Alamo, it remains in the possession of the Armstrong
family, of which Sarita is a member.*

1 cup mayonnaise
1/4 cup beef broth
2 cloves garlic
2 tablespoons capers
1 tablespoon dry mustard
1-1/2 teaspoons curry powder
Dash of Worcestershire sauce
Dash of Tabasco (or more)

In a blender, process all ingredients until
mixed. Serve as a salad dressing or as a dip
with vegetables.

MAKES ABOUT 1-1/2 CUPS

ninfa's green sauce

Ninfa's, an iconic restaurant in Houston, shared their recipe to be printed in the Houston Chronicle. The sauce is delicious with tortilla chips—especially fresh ones!—and a jar of it makes a nice homemade gift from the kitchen.

4 fresh tomatillos *or* 1 can (6 to 8 ounces)
   tomatillos, drained and chopped
3 medium green tomatoes, chopped
3 cloves garlic, minced
1 to 2 jalapeños, chopped
3 medium avocados, halved and seeded
1-1/2 cups (12 ounces) sour cream
1 tablespoon minced fresh cilantro
1/4 teaspoon salt

In a saucepan, simmer tomatillos, tomatoes, garlic and jalapeños for 15 minutes or until liquid has evaporated. Place avocados in a blender; add tomatillo mixture, sour cream, cilantro and salt. Blend for up to 5 minutes to create a smooth purée. Taste and add more salt if needed. Serve immediately with chips, or refrigerate until ready to serve.

SERVES 12-16

grundy family's favorite chocolate cake

LESTER GRUNDY

This old-fashioned cake travels well and has been requested by Will Grundy for his graduation party at Sewanee!

2 cups all-purpose flour
2 cups sugar
1/2 teaspoon salt
1/2 cup buttermilk
1/2 teaspoon baking soda
3/4 cup water
1/2 cup butter, cubed
1/2 cup canola *or* vegetable oil
1/4 cup baking cocoa
2 eggs, beaten
1 teaspoon ground cinnamon
1 teaspoon vanilla extract

icing:

1/2 cup butter, cubed
6 tablespoons buttermilk
1/4 cup cocoa
1 box (1 pound) powdered sugar, sifted
1 teaspoon vanilla extract

Preheat oven to 350°. In a mixing bowl, combine the flour, sugar and salt. In a small bowl, combine buttermilk and baking soda. In a saucepan over medium heat, bring water, butter, oil and cocoa just to a boil (watch it carefully). Pour over dry ingredients and mix. Add buttermilk and mix. Beat in eggs, cinnamon and vanilla. Line a greased and floured 13-inch x 9-inch x 2-inch baking pan with waxed paper; add batter. Bake for 25-30 minutes or until a toothpick comes out clean. Cool.

To make the icing: Combine butter, buttermilk and cocoa in a saucepan; bring to a boil. Add powdered sugar, a little at a time, beating with a wooden spoon between each addition so icing remains smooth. Once all of the sugar has been added, stir in vanilla. Spread over cooled cake.

SERVES 12-15

alice baker meyer's boston sugar cookies

GRAEME MARSTON

A Meyer family favorite. If you decide to decorate these with colored sugar, you can either buy colored sugar or tint your own with food coloring to get the colors you need.

1/2 cup butter, softened
1 cup sugar
2 tablespoons milk *or* cream
1 egg
1/2 teaspoon vanilla extract
1-3/4 cups all-purpose flour
2 teaspoons baking powder
1/2 teaspoon salt
Colored sugar in school colors, optional

With a mixer, cream butter and sugar until light. Beat in milk, egg and vanilla. Sift together the flour, baking powder and salt; add to creamed mixture and mix well. Shape into rolls; wrap in plastic wrap. Refrigerate until firm.

Preheat oven to 375°. Unwrap dough and cut into slices. Sprinkle with colored sugar if desired. Place on greased cookie sheets. Bake for 8-10 minutes. Remove to wire racks to cool. Store in tightly covered tins with waxed paper between layers.

mocha toffee bars

GAY ESTES

3 tablespoons instant espresso powder
2 tablespoons boiling water
1 cup unsalted butter, softened
1 cup packed brown sugar
1 egg yolk
1-1/2 teaspoons vanilla extract
2 cups all-purpose flour
1/2 teaspoon salt
8 ounces semisweet chocolate, melted
3/4 cup chopped unsalted roasted cashews

Preheat oven to 350°. Dissolve espresso powder in boiling water; set aside. With a mixer, cream butter and brown sugar until light and fluffy. Beat in egg yolk. Gradually add espresso and vanilla, beating until combined. Add flour and salt; beat until well combined.

Spread into a greased 15-inch x 10-inch x 1-inch baking pan. Bake for 15-20 minutes or until edges of bars pull away slightly from pan. Spread with melted chocolate; sprinkle with cashews. Cool on a wire rack. Cut into bars. Chill for 15-20 minutes or until chocolate is firm.

MAKES 4 DOZEN

HALLOWEEN

Halloween is such a magical time of year. Little ghoulies, ghosties and long-leggety beasties all delight in cruising the neighborhood for treats, and we have such fun creating parties for friends and neighbors. Pumpkin carving, pre- or post-trick- or-treat suppers, costume parties…the list of ways to come together for fun is endless as the shadows lengthen toward All Hallows Eve.

spider cake

DELBY WILLINGHAM

This is a great Halloween breakfast treat served with maple syrup. The cream in the cake forms a spiderweb. This recipe is from Herbert Smith, an old family retainer of the Willinghams in the Carolinas. He told children that he sat up all night trying to catch the spiders!

1 cup sugar
3/4 cup all-purpose flour
3/4 cup yellow cornmeal
1/2 teaspoon baking soda
1/2 teaspoon salt
1-1/2 teaspoons white vinegar
2 cups milk
1 tablespoon butter
1 cup heavy cream

Preheat oven to 350°. In a bowl, combine the sugar, flour, cornmeal, baking soda and salt. Add vinegar to milk; stir into dry ingredients. Melt butter in a baking pan or ovenproof skillet. (Herbert used a cast-iron frying pan.) Pour batter into center of pan. Pour cream on top; do not stir. Bake for 45 minutes or until golden brown. Serve with maple syrup.

halloween party memories ~ sara ledbetter

Almost annually for 10 years, my husband, Jim, and I hosted a pumpkin carving party for friends and family the Saturday before Halloween. Before we had children, we had the party in the evening, and we all drank wine and were creative.

When the kids were small, we held the party in the morning because young ones often fuss in the afternoon—better catch them early. As soon as the toddler stage was over, we moved the party to the cocktail hour to bring back some of that old hoopla.

Our inaugural year, we invited a few friends over and carved five pumpkins over dinner. We were living near downtown Houston in a patio home, which had a backyard the size of a 1970s bathroom. The last year we had the party, we had 300 people, a couple of scientists for slime making and dry-ice experiments, bartenders, cleaners and a fabulous fortune-teller!

The invitations were sometimes fun, sometimes a chore. One year, my father drew a fabulous pumpkin for the invite. Another year, we used a collage of pictures of old carved pumpkins from the party.

After the first few years, we established the tradition of taking our two youngsters to pick out pumpkins at the farmers market. I liked to buy a pumpkin for each invited child. The last year we had the party, two large SUVs caravanned to the market and we picked out close to 200 pumpkins, large and small.

The menu changed with the party, but Pumpkin Chocolate Chip Muffins were always a staple (the recipe is on the next page).

pumpkin chocolate chip muffins

SARA LEDBETTER

1-1/2 cups all-purpose flour
1 cup sugar
1 teaspoon pumpkin pie spice
1 teaspoon ground cinnamon
1 teaspoon baking soda
1/4 teaspoon baking powder
1/4 teaspoon salt
2 eggs
1 cup canned pumpkin
1/2 cup butter, melted
1 cup (6 ounces) semisweet chocolate chips

Preheat oven to 350°. In a large bowl, combine the first seven ingredients. In a separate bowl, beat the eggs, pumpkin and butter; add to dry ingredients and stir just until moistened. Fold in chocolate chips. Spoon into greased muffin cups. Bake for 20-25 minutes (10-15 for mini muffins) or until a toothpick comes out clean.

MAKES 1 DOZEN LARGE OR
1-1/2 DOZEN MINI MUFFINS

rose al-banna's gingerbread pumpkin trifle

KAREN TERRELL

Better if made a day ahead of time so gingersnaps soften...enjoy!

1 package (14.5 ounces) gingerbread cake mix
1 package (5.1 ounces) instant vanilla pudding
1 can (30 ounces) pumpkin pie mix
1 box (16 ounces) gingersnaps
1 carton (8 ounces) frozen whipped topping, thawed

Bake gingerbread cake according to package directions; cool. Prepare pudding according to package directions; let it thicken, then stir in the pumpkin pie mix. Cut cake into cubes. In a trifle dish, layer half of the cake cubes, pumpkin pudding, gingersnaps and whipped topping. Repeat layers. Decorate with whole gingersnaps.

SERVES 8-10

ghost whispers meringues

HARRIET POTTER

Scary good, but do not brown!

4 egg whites, room temperature
1/4 teaspoon cream of tartar
1/8 teaspoon salt
1 cup sugar
1 teaspoon vanilla extract
2 ounces chocolate candy bar *or* chips, melted

Preheat oven to 200°. With a mixer, beat egg whites, cream of tartar and salt on medium speed until fluffy. Slowly add sugar, a tablespoon at a time (this is the secret to fluffy cookies), beating until stiff. Beat in vanilla. Drop by teaspoonfuls onto a foil-lined cookie sheet. Bake for 1-1/2 to 2 hours or until dry. "Paint" on features with melted chocolate.

MAKES 4 DOZEN

more october 31st fun

Quick 'n' Easy Ghosts: When there isn't enough time to make meringues, Mimi Kerr creates ghosts with dollops of whipped topping and adds faces with icing gel.

"Finger Food": Mimi uses baby carrots, cream cheese, slivered almonds and red food coloring to make these ghoulish treats. First she tints the almonds with food coloring to look like fingernails, then she attaches them to the carrot tips with a dab of cream cheese.

Ol' Glove Trick: Robin Howell stuffs non-latex gloves with popcorn to look like creepy, lumpy hands.

Playful Prank: Meg Tapp's husband, Filson, took down their front door and put on a false front with a hole for the candy bowl. Trick-or-treaters were asked to ring the doorbell...at the sound of the bell, the family's dogs came running to the door and licked the child's hand!

chocolate popcorn

MIMI KERR

8 to 10 cups popped popcorn
1 cup (6 ounces) chocolate chips
12 large marshmallows, quartered
1/4 cup butter
1 tablespoon milk

Preheat oven to 300°. Place popcorn in a
very large bowl. In a heavy saucepan over low
heat, melt the chocolate chips, marshmallows
and butter. When melted and a thick syrup
forms, add milk to thin. Pour over popcorn
and toss until evenly coated. Spread on two
baking sheets. Bake for 5 minutes. Stir to
separate kernels; bake for 5 more minutes.
Cool on baking sheets, then toss to separate.

MAKES ABOUT 2 QUARTS

earthquake cake

MIKKI PHILLIPS

This cake is fun for family celebrations because, as its name suggests, you never know how it's going to look—it will be non-picture perfect, like an earthquake. It's a scrumptious trick or treat all in one!

1 cup flaked coconut
1 cup chopped pecans
1 package (18.25 ounces) German
   chocolate cake mix
1-1/2 teaspoons vanilla extract, *divided*
1/2 cup butter *or* 1/4 cup butter plus
   1/4 cup applesauce
1 box (1 pound) powdered sugar
Truffles, kisses *or* other chocolate candies

Preheat oven to 350°. Combine coconut and pecans; sprinkle over the bottom of one well-greased 16-inch x 9-1/2-inch glass baking dish or two 8-inch square glass baking dishes. Prepare cake batter as directed on box, adding 1 teaspoon vanilla. Spread batter over coconut and pecans.

Mix butter (or butter and applesauce), a bit less than the whole box of powdered sugar and remaining vanilla. Drop by large cooking spoonfuls over batter; do not mix. Bake as directed on cake box. When you take cake out of the oven, place chocolate candies on top and let them melt.

SERVES A CROWD

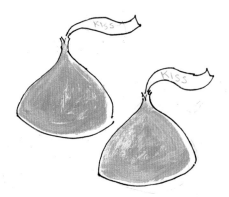

DAY OF THE DEAD ~ ALL SOULS DAY

Mariquita Masterson, the renowned jewelry designer, grew up in Mexico City. She has brought the traditions with her in a celebration of life called "Día de los Muertos" (Day of the Dead), known in the U.S. as All Saints or All Souls Day, November 1.

Celebrants set up an ofrenda—a shrine with mementos such as pictures, flowers, large wax candles in glasses (found in Latin American grocery stores), sugar skulls (calaveras) and pan de muerto ("bread of the dead"). The deceased's favorite foods and drinks are placed on the table. Giant marigolds (called cempasúchil by the Aztecs), which are in bloom in Mexico at the time, decorate the altars and doorways.

dead man's bread

MARIQUITA MASTERSON

2 packages (1/4 ounce *each*) active dry yeast
5 tablespoons warm milk (110° to 115°)
7-1/2 cups sifted flour
2 cups sugar
1 cup plus 2 tablespoons butter, cubed
12 small eggs
1 tablespoon lard
1 tablespoon ground cinnamon
2 teaspoons vanilla extract
1/2 cup milk

Preheat oven to 350°. Dissolve yeast in warm milk. Mound flour on counter or in a bowl and make a well in the center. Place the yeast and remaining ingredients in well. Work into dough and knead until dough pulls away from counter/bowl (if dough is too soft, knead in more flour). Shape into a ball; grease and flour it lightly and place in a greased bowl. Let rise in a warm place for 2-1/2 hours or until doubled. Cover with a towel and refrigerate overnight.

Shape dough into peach-size balls. Decorate the tops with strips of dough to look like bones. Place on greased baking sheets. Let rise in a warm place for 1-1/2 hours or until doubled. Dust with sugar. Bake for 30 minutes or until bottoms sound hollow when tapped.

To make a loaf: Instead of making balls, fill a loaf pan about two-thirds full with dough. Let rise for 1-1/2 hours. Bake for 40 minutes or until bottom sounds hollow when tapped.

MAKES 2-1/2 DOZEN ROLLS OR 1 LOAF

day of the dead fried bread with syrup

MARIQUITA MASTERSON

1 loaf day-old egg bread *or* Dead Man's Bread
  (see recipe on page 57)
2 cups warm milk
3 tablespoons plus 1/2 cup sugar, *divided*
2 cups water
1 cinnamon stick
1 star anise
1 cup white wine
3 eggs, lightly beaten
Vegetable oil

Cut bread into 3/4-inch slices; arrange in a deep bowl. Combine milk and 3 tablespoons sugar; pour over bread. Soak for 20 minutes. While the bread is soaking, make the syrup: In a saucepan, combine the water, cinnamon, anise and remaining sugar; simmer for 8 minutes. Stir in wine; simmer 5 more minutes. Cool slightly. Discard cinnamon stick and anise.

With a slotted spoon, remove each bread slice from milk mixture; dip in beaten eggs and fry in hot oil until golden. Drain on brown paper. Arrange fried bread slices on a serving platter and pour hot syrup over them.

perfect margarita

1-1/2 ounces silver tequila
1/2 ounce orange liqueur (Controy from
  Mexico, Cointreau *or* Triple Sec)
1 ounce fresh lime juice

Shake all ingredients over ice or blend with ice for a frozen margarita. For authenticity, wet the rim of the glass in lime juice and dip in a dish of salt.

mango margarita

2 ounces tequila
1/2 teaspoon orange liqueur (Controy from
  Mexico, Cointreau *or* Triple Sec)
6 ounces mango juice*

Shake all ingredients over ice or blend with ice for a frozen margarita. For authenticity, wet the rim of the glass in water or juice and dip in a dish of salt.

* Look for mango juice in boxes in the juice section of your grocery store.

Peeled and sliced jicama, sprinkled with cayenne pepper and fresh lime juice, makes a tasty hors d'oeuvres. Keep the tubers in ice water until covering with lime juice. This is a "New" Mexico treat served in Santa Fe. Spicy!

red tamales

MARIQUITA MASTERSON

Look for masa harina and dried corn husks at Mexican or Latin food markets. Serve these with cerveza "bien fria" (very cold beer) or margaritas!

1 pound boneless pork, cut into chunks
4 cloves garlic, *divided*
1 onion, chopped
2 ounces ancho chiles, seeds removed
2 cups hot water
1 tablespoon lard
2 pounds masa harina
3/4 cup plus 2 tablespoons lard
3/4 cup plus 2 tablespoons baking powder
1 tablespoon salt
40 dried corn husks, soaked in cold water
   and drained well

Place pork in a saucepan with enough water to cover; add 2 garlic cloves and onion. Cover and cook until tender, about 45 minutes. Drain, reserving broth. Shred the meat and set aside. Soak the chiles in hot water for 10 minutes; purée with remaining garlic. Sauté purée in hot lard for 3 minutes. Add shredded pork; season with salt to taste. Cook for 3 minutes or until thickened.

In a mixing bowl, beat masa harina with 1 cup reserved pork broth for 10 minutes. In another bowl, beat lard thoroughly until spongy. Add to masa with baking powder and salt; beat well. Spread 1 tablespoonful on each corn husk; top with a small amount of pork filling. Fold long edges of husks toward center to enclose filling, then fold the ends up to shape each tamale into a tightly wrapped package.

Pour water into a large steamer. Place a layer of extra corn husks on the bottom; stand filled tamales upright around the edge of the steamer. Cover and steam for 1 hour or until tamales are cooked through. To test, remove and open a tamale—the filling should separate easily from the husk.

SERVES 8-10

tamales in banana leaves

MARIQUITA MASTERSON

1 pound boneless pork *or* chicken
2 onions, *divided*
2 cloves garlic, *divided*
Salt
1 tablespoon corn oil
2 cups puréed tomatoes, drained
3 tablespoons chopped fresh cilantro
1/2 cup lard, *divided*
1 pound masa harina
3 large banana leaves

Place meat in a saucepan with enough water
to cover; add 1 onion, cut in half, 1 garlic
clove and salt to taste. Cook slowly until very
tender. Cool, drain and shred; set aside.
Finely chop the second onion and mince the
second garlic clove. Heat oil in a large sauté
pan; sauté onion and garlic until translucent.
Add shredded meat; sauté for 2 minutes.
Add the tomatoes, cilantro and salt to taste.
Simmer for 10 minutes or until thickened.

Set aside 2 tablespoons of lard. In a mixing
bowl, beat masa harina with remaining
lard and salt to taste for 5 minutes or until
spongy. Hold the banana leaves over an open
flame for a few seconds until they soften and
become pliable. Cut 1 large leaf into 6-inch
squares. Grease outside surface of the squares
with reserved lard. Place a portion of masa
on each square; top with 1-1/2 tablespoons
meat filling. Fold edges of squares toward the
center, enclosing filling and making a tightly
wrapped rectangular package. You can tie
each one with a strip of leaf.

Place remaining banana leaves on the bottom
of a large steamer; cover leaves with water.
Stand filled tamales upright around the edge
of the steamer. Cover and steam for 1 hour
or until tamales are cooked through. To test,
remove and open a tamale—the filling should
separate easily from the husk.

SERVES 8-10

tortillas dolce

MIMI KERR

10 flour tortillas
Melted butter
2/3 cup sugar
1-3/4 teaspoons cinnamon

Preheat oven to 450°. Place tortillas on
foil-lined baking sheets. Brush generously
with butter. Combine sugar and cinnamon;
sprinkle over tortillas. Bake for 4-5 minutes
or until crisp and bubbly.

SERVES 5

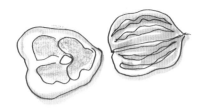

mexican wedding cookies

GAY ESTES

1 cup butter, softened
3/4 cup powdered sugar
1 teaspoon black walnut flavoring
2 cups all-purpose flour
1/4 teaspoon salt
1 cup chopped walnuts *or* pecans
Additional powdered sugar

Preheat oven to 325°. With a mixer, cream
butter and powdered sugar. Beat in flavoring,
flour and salt until combined. Stir in nuts.
Roll into small balls. Place on cookie sheets.
Bake for 20 minutes. Roll warm cookies in
powdered sugar; cool and roll again.

MAKES ABOUT 1-1/2 DOZEN

VETERANS DAY

Formerly called Armistice Day, Veterans Day is celebrated on November 11. People wore red poppies to commemorate those who died in service to their country.

anzac biscuits

VERLINDE DOUBLEDAY

Named after the combined military forces of Australia and New Zealand, Anzac biscuits became the national cookie of those two countries. Verlinde Doubleday's in-laws came from New Zealand, as did this recipe.

1 cup oats
1 cup sugar
1 cup all-purpose flour
3/4 cup flaked coconut
3/4 cup butter
1 tablespoon pure cane syrup
   (such as Steen's)
1 teaspoon baking soda
2 tablespoons boiling water

Preheat oven to 325°. In a large bowl, combine the oats, sugar, flour and coconut. Gently melt butter and syrup together. Dissolve baking soda in boiling water; add to butter mixture. Gently add to the dry ingredients. Form into marble-size balls. Place on parchment paper-lined cookie sheets, allowing room for spreading. Bake for 9-12 minutes. Cool before removing from pan.

MAKES ABOUT 2 DOZEN

*Hunting season brings fresh wild game, including venison, duck, fish and fowl.
There is always enough to share with hunting buddies and good friends. A child
at House of Pooh Corner thought that Hunting Season was the fifth season!
Many grown-ups do, too, so we added a game section.*

katherine shanks dodd's braised duck

DELBY WILLINGHAM

1 to 2 ducks
2 leeks (white portion only), sliced
3 ribs celery with leaves, chopped
3 carrots, chopped
1/2 cup chopped fresh parsley
3 cloves garlic, minced
2 bay leaves
2 tablespoons dried thyme
Salt and pepper
6 bacon strips, chopped
2 onions, coarsely chopped
1 tablespoon butter
4 to 5 tablespoons all-purpose flour
18 pearl onions
1 small package baby carrots

Parboil ducks in water to cover for 2 hours (depending on size). Reserve cooking water; reserve giblets for gravy. Add the leeks, celery, carrots, parsley, garlic, bay leaves, thyme, salt and pepper. Simmer for 1-1/2 hours.

Strain stock and discard vegetables. Cut duck into pieces; place in a glass baking dish. Preheat oven to 325°. Fry bacon with onions until golden brown. Drain on paper towel; sprinkle over duck. Add butter to bacon drippings; brown flour. Add giblets and enough stock to make gravy to cover duck pieces. (Strain and freeze remaining stock for soup.) Cover and bake for 30 minutes. Add pearl onions and baby carrots; bake 30 minutes longer. Serve over wild rice with cranberry sauce on the side.

Wine Recommendation: Brennan Vineyards Syrah

armstrong ranch carne guisada

SARITA HIXON

This is another recipe from the famous Armstrong Ranch in South Texas. Nilgai is a type of antelope hunted at the ranch.

1 tablespoon vegetable oil
1-1/4 pounds meat (beef, venison *or* nilgai), cut into bite-size pieces
2 to 3 tablespoons all-purpose flour
1-1/2 cups beef stock *or* 1 can (14 ounces) beef broth
1 medium onion, chopped
2 jalapeños *or* Serranos, minced
1 tablespoon tomato paste
3 teaspoons ground cumin
1 teaspoon chili powder (or more)

Preheat oven to 350°. Heat oil over high heat in a heavy ovenproof skillet or Dutch oven; brown meat quickly (in batches if necessary). Once all the meat is browned, dust lightly with flour and return to the pan. Stir in the remaining ingredients. Bring to a simmer on the stove. Cover and bake for 2½ hours or until meat is falling-apart tender. This freezes well and just needs to be reheated when thawed.

SERVES 3-4 AS A MAIN DISH OR 4-6 IN TACOS

watercress salad

MARY TRAINER

Our family favorite. You can cut the vinaigrette ingredients in half, or refrigerate the leftovers for another time. And you can toast the almonds in butter if you like.

2-1/2 cups olive oil
3 to 6 tablespoons champagne vinegar
3/4 teaspoon dry mustard
1 tablespoon chopped onion
9 shakes pepper
4 to 6 bunches of watercress (top 3 inches of each bunch)
1-1/2 pounds sliced fresh mushrooms
3 cups sliced hearts of palm
1-1/2 cups slivered almonds, toasted

For vinaigrette, blend the oil, vinegar, mustard, onion and pepper in a blender. Arrange the watercress, mushrooms and hearts of palm on a serving platter or individual salad plates; sprinkle with almonds and drizzle with desired amount of vinaigrette. Refrigerate remaining vinaigrette for another use.

beth's cornbread

KAREN TERRELL

2 eggs
1/2 cup vegetable oil
1 cup (8 ounces) sour cream
1 can (7 ounces) creamed corn
1 cup cornbread mix

Preheat oven to 375°. In a bowl, whisk the eggs, oil and sour cream. Add corn. Stir in cornmeal mix just until blended. Pour into a greased 8-inch square baking pan. Bake for 30-40 minutes or until golden.

SERVES 6-8

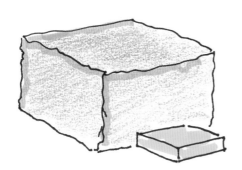

wild rice casserole

MARY TRAINER

1 cup uncooked wild rice
1 cup sliced ripe olives
1 cup canned tomatoes with juice
1 cup sliced fresh mushrooms
1/2 cup chopped onion
1/2 cup vegetable oil
Salt and pepper to taste
1/2 cup hot water
1 cup (4 ounces) shredded cheddar cheese

Soak rice overnight; drain. Preheat oven to 350°. Combine the rice, olives, tomatoes, mushrooms, onion, oil, salt and pepper; place in a buttered casserole dish. Add hot water. Cover and bake for 1-1/2 hours. Check occasionally toward end of baking time to ensure rice is not drying out; add more hot water if needed. Rice should be tender. Before serving, sprinkle cheese on top; cover and let stand until cheese melts.

SERVES 6

carrot soufflé

FRANCITA ULMER

2 cups (1 pound) carrots
2 teaspoons lemon juice
3 eggs, lightly beaten
1 cup milk
1/2 cup butter, softened
1/4 cup sugar
2 tablespoons minced onion
1 tablespoon all-purpose flour
1 teaspoon sugar
1/2 teaspoon ground cinnamon
1/2 teaspoon ground cloves

Preheat oven to 350°. Cook and purée the carrots; add lemon juice. Place in a mixing bowl. Add the remaining ingredients; beat until smooth. Transfer to a buttered 2-quart baking dish. Bake for 45-60 minutes or until firm. Can assemble the day before and refrigerate overnight, then bake it the next day.

SERVES 6-8

margaret drumm carlisle's molded cranberry orange salad

ELIZABETH ROYCE

6 cups fresh cranberries
3 large navel oranges
1 cup sugar
3 envelopes (1/4 ounce *each*)
   unflavored gelatin
2 cups cold water
3 packages (3 ounces *each*) raspberry gelatin
4 cups boiling water
1/2 cup frozen orange juice, optional

In a food processor, grind cranberries in batches. Transfer to a large bowl. Remove stem area on end of oranges; cut each orange into 8 pieces. Grind oranges (rind and all); add to cranberries. Stir in sugar; let stand for 1 hour. Dissolve unflavored gelatin in cold water. In a large bowl, dissolve raspberry gelatin in boiling water; stir in unflavored gelatin. Add orange juice if desired. Stir in cranberry mixture. Pour into a mold that you've coated with cooking spray. Refrigerate until firm.

THANKSGIVING

*Our members have much for which to be grateful…this occasion, along with
Christmas, had the most contributed recipes.*

Thanksgiving Dinner Olé ~ Mary Nell Lovett

I started a tradition when my husband, Malcolm, and I were blessed with the first of our five grandchildren. When each of them came home from the hospital, summer or winter, I fixed a traditional Thanksgiving dinner for our daughters and sons-in-laws so we could celebrate our thankfulness.

Everyone seems to have a primal loyalty to her own stuffing or dressing recipe. When Thanksgiving rolls around, it's a "draw" with my family whether to have a traditional turkey dinner, with the "must-have" dressing, or a Mexican turkey dinner.

The menu for our Thanksgiving Dinner Olé features: fried oysters with pico de gallo and mango salsa for appetizers...Turkey with Tamale Stuffing and Enchilada Gravy...Muy Bueno Black Beans...Light Spanish Rice...Avocado, Ruby Reds and Jicama Salad...jalapeño and/or plain corn muffins or corn sticks...and Texas pecan pie and pralines 'n' cream à la mode for dessert.

turkey with tamale stuffing and enchilada gravy

1 turkey (12 to 16 pounds)

gravy:

2-1/2 cans (10 ounces *each*) mild enchilada sauce (such as Gebhardts)

2 cans water

2 cans (14 ounces *each*) chicken broth (or use homemade stock)

1 medium onion, quartered

1 clove garlic, peeled

2 teaspoons chili powder

1 teaspoon salt

1/2 teaspoon poultry seasoning

Turkey liver, gizzard and neck

stuffing:

8 ounces bulk seasoned sausage

1 medium onion, chopped

1/4 cup butter

48 tamales

1 pan (9-inch square) day-old cornbread

2 eggs, beaten

1/2 can mild enchilada sauce (such as Gebhardts)

1/2 teaspoon ground cumin

1/4 teaspoon cayenne pepper

Salt and pepper to taste

Combine the gravy ingredients and simmer for 3-4 hours, adding more water if necessary. Strain before use. Best made the day ahead.

To make the stuffing: Brown sausage and drain if necessary. Sauté onion in butter. Crumble tamales and cornbread into a large bowl. Add sausage, onion and remaining ingredients; mix gently. Loosely stuff turkey and truss before baking. Place any extra dressing in a greased casserole. Bake turkey at 325° for 3-4 hours, basting frequently with enchilada gravy, until a meat ther-mometer reads 180°. Bake extra dressing for about 30 minutes while turkey is out of oven and resting.

SERVES 8-12

muy bueno
black beans

I tend to use more of each spice when making this recipe. It's best made ahead and reheated, which comes in handy during the busy holiday season.

1 pound dried black beans
8-1/2 cups water, *divided*
1/2 pound bacon, diced
1 cup chopped onion
1 clove garlic, minced

2-1/2 cups water
3/4 teaspoon dried oregano
1/2 teaspoon dried rosemary, crushed
1/2 teaspoon ground cumin
1/4 teaspoon dried thyme
1/4 teaspoon pepper
1 can (28 ounces) diced tomatoes
Salt to taste

Bring beans and 6 cups water to a boil for 2 minutes. Remove from the heat; let it sit, covered, for 1 hour. In a large pot, cook bacon until golden brown; remove the bacon. Drain all but 2 tablespoons of the drippings. In the drippings, sauté onion and garlic until tender. Add the seasonings and remaining water. Drain the beans. Add beans and bacon to the pot. Simmer for 1-1/2 hours or until tender. Add tomatoes with their liquid and salt if needed. Simmer for 30 more minutes. Add more water if necessary while cooking.

SERVES 12-14

light spanish rice

I serve rice and beans in separate serving dishes. Or I'll pack rice into a ring mold, then unmold it and place a bowl of beans in the hole for presentation.

1/2 cup chopped green pepper
1/2 cup chopped onion
1 can (16 ounces) tomato sauce
1 can (14.5 ounces) stewed tomatoes, undrained and chopped
1 cup uncooked long-grain white rice
1/4 cup water
1 teaspoon chili powder
1/2 teaspoon dried oregano
1/4 teaspoon salt
1/4 teaspoon ground red pepper
1/4 teaspoon ground cumin

Lightly coat a large skillet with cooking spray and place over medium-high heat until hot. Add green pepper and onion; sauté for 5 minutes or until tender. Add the remaining ingredients; bring to a boil. Cover; reduce heat and simmer for 25-30 minutes or until rice is tender and liquid is absorbed.

SERVES 8

avocado, ruby reds and jicama salad

This salad is versatile—by varying the amounts of fruits and veggies, you can easily serve a few people or a large group.

Jicama, peeled and cut into matchstick pieces
Fresh lime *or* grapefruit juice
Mixed salad greens
Avocados, peeled and sliced
Ruby Red grapefruit, peeled and sectioned
Your choice of dressing: oil 'n' vinegar, cilantro-lime *or* poppy seed

Toss jicama pieces with lime or grapefruit juice. Arrange salad greens on a platter or individual salad plates; fan the avocados, grapefruit and jicama over greens. Drizzle with dressing.

Wine Recommendation for this menu: for red, Becker Vineyards Cabernet Sauvignon, French Burgundy, Oregon Pinot Noir or Beaujolais...for white, Riesling, Vouvray or Gewürztraminer

quick "rolls"

LYDIA HILLIARD

2-1/4 cups biscuit mix, *divided*
1 cup (8 ounces) sour cream
1/2 cup butter, melted

Preheat oven to 350°. In a bowl, combine 2 cups biscuit mix, sour cream and butter; stir well. Sprinkle remaining biscuit mix on a flat surface, breaking up any large lumps. Drop batter by tablespoonfuls onto the biscuit mix; roll into 36 balls. Place 3 balls each into 12 greased muffin cups. Bake for 20-25 minutes or until golden brown.

MAKES 1 DOZEN

elmira's cornbread

LUCY GOODRICH

2 cups cornmeal mix
1 cup all-purpose flour
1 tablespoon baking powder
1 teaspoon salt
2 eggs, lightly beaten
1 cup milk

Preheat oven to 350°. In a bowl, combine the dry ingredients. Add eggs and milk; blend until just mixed. Pour into an 8- or 9-inch square pan. Bake for 20-25 minutes or until top is light brown. *Note:* There is no fat in this recipe as it is added in the dressing recipe.

elmira's cornmeal dressing

LUCY GOODRICH

1 recipe of Elmira's Cornbread
4 ribs celery, finely chopped
1 bunch green onions, chopped
1 red bell pepper, finely chopped
2 cloves garlic, minced
1 cup butter
2 eggs, beaten
2 cans (14 ounces *each*) chicken broth
Salt and white pepper to taste

Preheat oven to 350°. Crumble cornbread into a large bowl. Sauté the celery, green onions, red pepper and garlic in butter until translucent. Add to cornbread and mix well. Add eggs, broth, salt and pepper; stir well. Transfer to a baking dish. Bake for 1 hour or until lightly browned.

fruit chutney

BETTY DAVIS

12 tart apples, pears, peaches *or* mangoes,
   peeled and sliced
2 large green bell peppers, seeded
   and quartered
2 large onions, quartered
I can (4 ounces) whole green chiles, seeded
3 cloves garlic
1/2 cup peeled fresh gingerroot
3-1/2 cups packed brown sugar
2-1/2 cups cider vinegar
1-1/2 cups golden raisins
2 teaspoons salt
1/2 teaspoon cayenne pepper

In a food processor, chop the fruit, green
peppers, onions, chiles, garlic and ginger
until fine. Pour into a saucepan; add the
remaining ingredients. Cook, uncovered,
over low heat for 3 hours, stirring
occasionally.

cornbread dressing

MARGARET PIERCE

(adapted from Helen Corbett and the
recipe the Millers have always used)

8 cups crumbled cornbread*
1/2 cup finely chopped onion
1/2 cup finely chopped green bell pepper
1/2 cup finely chopped celery
3/4 cup butter
6 hard-boiled eggs, chopped
1/2 cup diced pimientos
1/2 cup minced fresh parsley
Salt and pepper to taste
Chicken stock to moisten

Preheat oven to 350°. Place cornbread in a
large bowl. Sauté onion, green pepper and
celery in butter. Add to cornbread. Stir in
eggs, pimientos and parsley. Season with salt
and pepper; moisten with stock. Spoon into
a buttered shallow glass baking dish. Bake for
30 minutes or until warmed through and
browned on top.

*Make two boxes of cornbread mix; bake until well
browned. Crumble and measure.*

frozen cranberry salad

CINDY WALLACE

This is my mother's frozen cranberry salad, which we have made since forever to go with Thanksgiving turkey. I think it would also be good with roast chicken or beef tenderloin. Even people who "don't like cranberry sauce" like this salad, and it is a little unusual and fun on a holiday buffet. It's a no-fail hit with children, because it tastes like dessert!

6 ounces cream cheese, softened
2 tablespoons mayonnaise
2 tablespoons sugar
1 can (16 ounces) whole-berry
   cranberry sauce
1 can (8 ounces) crushed pineapple, drained
1/2 cup chopped pecans
1 cup heavy cream
1 cup sifted powdered sugar
1 teaspoon vanilla extract

In a large bowl, combine the cream cheese, mayonnaise and sugar until smooth. Stir in cranberry sauce, pineapple and pecans. Beat cream until foamy; gradually add powdered sugar, beating until soft peaks form. Add vanilla. Fold into the cranberry-cream cheese mixture. Spoon into a 13-inch x 9-inch x 2-inch dish. Cover and freeze until firm. Cut into squares to serve.

SERVES 12

cranberry salsa

MIMI KERR

Delicious served with turkey and dressing or roasted pork.

1 package (16 ounces) fresh cranberries
1/2 to 3/4 cup sugar
1 cup chopped fresh cilantro
1 bunch green onions, finely chopped
1 to 2 jalapeños, seeded and finely diced
Juice of 1 lime
1 tablespoon olive oil
Salt and pepper to taste

In a food processor and using the chopping blade, coarsely chop the cranberries with sugar, being sure to not overgrind. Add the cilantro, green onions, jalapeños, lime juice and oil; pulse until combined. Taste and season with salt and pepper.

pumpkin cheesecake

MARY TRAINER

To make the crumbs for the crust, pulse graham crackers in a food processor until finely ground. Or you can substitute purchased graham cracker crumbs.

1-1/4 cups graham cracker crumbs
  (from 10 whole crackers)
1/4 cup sugar
1/4 cup unsalted butter, melted

filling:

4 packages (8 ounces *each*) cream
  cheese, softened
1-1/4 cups sugar
3 tablespoons all-purpose flour
1 cup canned pumpkin
2 tablespoons pumpkin pie spice
1 tablespoon vanilla extract
1/2 teaspoon salt
4 eggs, lightly beaten

Preheat oven to 350°, with rack in center. Assemble a 9-inch nonstick springform pan, with the raised side of the bottom part facing up.

To make the crust: Mix the graham cracker crumbs, sugar and butter until moistened; press firmly onto bottom of pan. Bake for 10-12 minutes or until golden around edges.

With a mixer, beat cream cheese and sugar on low speed until smooth; mix in flour (do not overmix). Add pumpkin, pie spice, vanilla and salt; mix just until smooth. Add eggs; beat on low speed just until blended.

Place springform pan on a rimmed baking sheet. Pour filling into pan and gently smooth top. Place in oven; reduce heat to 300°. Bake for 45 minutes. Turn off oven; let cheesecake stay in oven for 2 hours (without opening oven door). Remove from oven; cool completely. Cover with plastic wrap; refrigerate until firm, at least 4 hours. Remove sides of pan before serving.

SERVES 12

apple crisp with brandy

MARGARET GRIFFITH

6 Granny Smith apples
1/2 cup sugar
2 teaspoons lemon juice
1 teaspoon ground cinnamon
1/2 teaspoon ground coriander seeds
1/8 teaspoon ground cloves
1/2 cup coarsely chopped walnuts *or* pecans
3 tablespoons Calvados *or* other brandy

3/4 cup sifted all-purpose flour
1/2 cup sugar
6 tablespoons cold butter
Heavy cream *or* ice cream

Preheat oven to 350°. Peel, core and slice the apples. Toss with sugar, lemon juice, spices and nuts. Put the mixture in a buttered shallow casserole. Sprinkle with Calvados. In a bowl, mix flour and sugar; cut in butter with a pastry blender or with your fingers until the mixture is crumbly. Sprinkle over apples. Bake for 40 minutes or until filling is bubbly and topping is browned. If the top is not brown enough, increase the oven temperature to 425° for the last 5 minutes. Serve warm with cream or ice cream.

SERVES 4-6

butternut crème brûlée

GAIL HENDRYX

A nice change from pumpkin pie on Thanksgiving.

3 cups heavy cream
1/2 cup sugar
6 egg yolks
1/3 cup puréed cooled butternut squash
1/4 teaspoon ground cinnamon

1/8 teaspoon ground ginger
Pinch ground cloves
1 tablespoon dark rum
1/3 cup packed light brown sugar

Preheat oven to 325°. Heat cream and sugar in a double boiler until sugar has dissolved. Remove from the heat. With a mixer, beat egg yolks until light. Add squash, cinnamon, ginger and cloves. Whisk in the hot cream mixture. Stir in the rum. Pour into a 1-1/2-quart soufflé dish. Place dish in a roasting pan; add boiling water to come halfway up the sides of the soufflé dish. Bake for 1 to 1-1/2 hours or until center is fairly firm.

Remove pan from the water bath and allow to cool. Refrigerate overnight. About 15 minutes before serving, preheat the broiler. Sprinkle brown sugar over the custard. Place the dish in a baking pan and surround it with ice cubes. Heat in the broiler, gently shaking the pan until the sugar melts. Serve immediately.

SERVES 6-8

BLACK FRIDAY

*That funny day after Thanksgiving is for shopping and re-enjoying
yesterday's feast. These delicious recipes deserve a place of their own,
never known as mere leftovers.*

chipotle turkey salad

GAY ESTES

1 cup chopped cooked turkey
1/4 cup chopped onion
1/4 cup chopped celery
1/4 cup mayonnaise
1 tablespoon fresh *or* canned chopped
   jalapeños (or to taste)
1 tablespoon chopped fresh cilantro
1/4 to 1/2 teaspoon chipotle chili powder
Salt and pepper to taste

Just mix and serve on greens, or make a
sandwich.

SERVES 1-2

black friday
chili blanco

MARY TRAINER

1 cup chopped onion
2 tablespoons minced garlic
1/4 cup vegetable oil
1 tablespoon ground cumin (or to taste)
2 pounds boneless skinless turkey breasts,
   cut into 3/4-inch cubes
1 pound ground turkey
6 cups chicken broth
2 cans (15 ounces *each*) chickpeas,
   rinsed and drained
2/3 cup pearl barley
1 tablespoon canned chopped
   jalapeños (or to taste)
1 teaspoon dried marjoram
1/2 teaspoon dried savory, crumbled
1-1/2 tablespoons cornstarch
1/2 cup cold water
Salt and pepper to taste
4 cups (16 ounces) shredded
   Monterey Jack cheese
1/2 cup thinly sliced scallions

In a large pot, cook and stir the onion and garlic in oil over medium heat until onion is translucent. Add cumin; cook and stir for 5 minutes. Add cubed and ground turkey; cook over medium heat until meat is no longer pink. Stir in the broth, chickpeas, barley, jalapeños, marjoram and savory. Cover and simmer for 45 minutes, stirring occasionally. Dissolve cornstarch in water; stir into the chili. Simmer, uncovered, for 15 minutes. Season with salt and pepper. To serve, top with cheese and scallions.

SERVES 8-10

black friday turkey mulligatawny soup

GINGER CURRIE

Turkey carcass broken into large pieces
4 to 5 quarts water
4 cloves garlic
3 cubes (1 inch) peeled fresh gingerroot
1/3 cup cold water
1/4 cup canola oil
2 tablespoons curry powder
3/4 teaspoon ground cumin
2 large boiling potatoes (about 1 pound),
    peeled and cubed
4 cups chopped onions
3 carrots, sliced
1/2 to 1 cup canned unsweetened
    coconut milk
1/4 cup fresh lime juice (or to taste)
1/3 cup chopped fresh cilantro plus sprigs
    for garnish
Salt and freshly ground pepper to taste

Place turkey carcass in a large pot; add
enough water to cover, 4 to 5 quarts.
Simmer, uncovered, for 3 hours. Strain
through a sieve; return stock to the pot.
Boil until reduced to 10 cups.

In a food processor, purée garlic and ginger
with cold water. In an iron skillet, heat oil
over medium-high heat until it is hot but not
smoking. Add the purée; cook and stir for
2 minutes or until liquid is just evaporated.
Add curry powder and cumin; cook and stir
for 1 minute. Transfer mixture to a soup pot
or large saucepan.

Add the potatoes, onions, carrots and 5 cups
stock. Cover and simmer for 30 minutes
or until vegetables are very soft. Meanwhile,
remove turkey meat from the carcass; set
aside. Stir remaining stock into soup. Add
coconut milk, lime juice, chopped cilantro,
salt and pepper. Simmer for 10 more
minutes. To serve, place turkey in soup
bowls; ladle soup into bowls and top with
a cilantro sprig.

SERVES 10

black friday enchiladas

GAY ESTES

2 cups spicy *or* mild salsa, *divided*

1 to 2 limes

4 cups shredded cooked turkey

Salt and pepper to taste

2 cups mashed cooked sweet potatoes

Pinch of ground cumin

2 cans (4 ounces *each*) chopped roasted
green chiles, drained, *divided*

12 corn tortillas

Olive oil

1-1/2 cups (6 ounces) shredded
Monterey Jack cheese

Preheat oven to 350°. Pour 1 cup salsa into
a 13-inch x 9-inch x 2-inch baking pan.
Squeeze limes onto turkey and stir; sprinkle
with salt and pepper. Season sweet potatoes
with cumin and add 1 can of chiles. In a
skillet, soften tortillas in oil. Place a spoonful
of turkey and sweet potatoes on each tortilla
and wrap up. Lay filled tortillas on salsa.
Top with second can of chiles and remaining
salsa. Sprinkle with shredded cheese. Bake
for 30 minutes or until bubbly.

SERVES 6-8

clementine salad

GAIL HENDRYX

*Clementines are small sweet tangerines available in winter.
In this recipe, pepper is a wonderful offset to the fruit's
sweetness while the avocados are a foil for their acidity.
And because of that acidity, you don't need the usual acid
portion of salad dressing—just the olive oil.*

8 clementines

Fresh coarsely ground pepper

4 ripe avocados, cut into slender slices

Pinch of salt

Olive oil (lemon-flavored if available)

Spinach leaves, optional

Peel clementines and divide into segments.
Vigorously apply coarse pepper—you should
see it plainly. Add avocados, salt and a touch
of olive oil; mix gently and serve. If you
wish, you may pile it in the middle of a plate
of spinach.

SERVES 4

apple crisp

VERLINDE DOUBLEDAY

*This is such a quick, easy and delicious dessert, that
yes—you can make it the day after Thanksgiving!*

5 cups thinly sliced peeled Granny
    Smith apples
1 cup all-purpose flour
1-1/3 cups sugar (mix of white and
    dark brown sugar)
2/3 teaspoon salt
1 teaspoon ground cinnamon
2/3 cup butter, melted

Preheat oven to 350°. Put apples in a greased
13-inch x 9-inch x 2-inch baking pan. In
a bowl, combine the flour, sugar, salt and
cinnamon; add butter and mix well. Spread
over apples. Bake for 45-50 minutes or until
golden and bubbly.

SERVES 4-6

FALL FAVORITES

The wonderful palette and flavors of autumn are inspiring to the cook!

Harvest Supper ~ Mimi Lloyd

I created and prepared this menu in honor of our visiting Wallace Lecture Speaker, Wendy Andrade. The Wallace Lecture is open to the public and is a demonstration of distinguished flower arrangers held at the Houston Museum of Fine Arts.

The menu featured: Chutney Cream Cheese Spread, Pumpkin Biscuits, Grilled Dijon-Marinated Pork Tenderloin with Ginger Applesauce, Sweet Potato Pancakes, Mixed Winter Squash Provençal and Pumpkin Spice Cake.

chutney cream cheese spread

3 packages (8 ounces *each*) cream
  cheese, softened
3 tablespoons medium-dry sherry
3 tablespoons light brown sugar
1 tablespoon best-quality curry powder
1 tablespoon ground ginger
1 teaspoon dry mustard
1 bunch scallions, trimmed and minced
6 ounces mango chutney, finely chopped
6 ounces sharp cheddar cheese, shredded
Grated zest of 1 lime
6 ounces hickory-smoked almonds,
  coarsely chopped
Your choice of fruits (such as grapes,
  oranges, apples, pears, kumquats),
  cut into bite-size pieces
Crackers if serving as a spread
Toasted coconut

With a mixer, beat the cream cheese, sherry,
brown sugar, curry, ginger and mustard.
Stir in scallions, chutney, cheddar, lime zest
and almonds. Let the flavors mellow for a
few hours in the refrigerator. Serve at room
temperature, spooned into bite-size pieces
of fruit, or as a spread with crackers. Garnish
with coconut.

pumpkin seed biscuits

2 tablespoons pumpkin seeds
2 cups all-purpose flour
4 teaspoons baking powder
1 tablespoon sugar
1 teaspoon salt
1/4 teaspoon cream of tartar
1/2 cup cold unsalted butter, cut into pieces
2/3 cup plus 1 tablespoon buttermilk
1 egg white, lightly beaten

In a small skillet over medium heat, toast the
pumpkin seeds, shaking the pan frequently
until all are golden brown and beginning to
pop, about 6 minutes. Set aside. Preheat the
oven to 400°.

In a large bowl, combine the flour, baking
powder, sugar, salt and cream of tartar.
Using your fingers or a pastry cutter, cut in
butter until mixture is the consistency of
coarse cornmeal. Carefully mix in buttermilk
until just incorporated (mixture will appear
crumbly). Turn onto a lightly floured surface. Gently press the dough into a 3/4-inch
disk; cut out 12 biscuits with a biscuit cutter.

Place on a parchment paper-lined baking sheet. Lightly brush tops with egg white; sprinkle with toasted pumpkin seeds. Bake for 12 minutes or until golden brown. Serve warm.

MAKES 1 DOZEN

grilled dijon-marinated pork tenderloin with ginger applesauce

1/2 cup Dijon mustard
2 cloves garlic, minced
1/4 teaspoon white pepper
4 small pork tenderloins (about
  1/2 pound *each*)

applesauce:

5 large Granny Smith apples, peeled,
  cored and quartered
8 pieces (1/2 inch thick) fresh
  gingerroot, peeled
3 ounces crystallized ginger, minced
1 tablespoon olive oil
1 onion, finely chopped
1 tablespoon sugar (or to taste)
Salt and pepper to taste

In a glass baking dish, combine the mustard, garlic and pepper. Add the tenderloins and turn to coat. Cover and refrigerate for 6-12 hours.

To make the applesauce: Place apples and fresh ginger in a saucepan; add enough water to cover. Simmer until apples are tender, less than 10 minutes. Careful! Remove pieces of ginger. Strain out the liquid. Place cooked apples and crystallized ginger in a food processor; pulse until slightly chunky. In a small saucepan, heat oil on medium-low. Sauté onion for 20 minutes or until soft and caramelized. Add to apple mixture. Season with sugar, salt and pepper.

Grill pork on a medium-hot grill for 10-15 minutes, turning occasionally, or until a meat thermometer reads 155°. Let stand for 5 minutes; slice into 1/4-inch-thick medallions. Serve with applesauce.

SERVES 8

sweet potato pancakes

5 medium sweet potatoes, peeled
1 bunch scallions, trimmed and minced
1/2 cup crushed gingersnap crumbs
3 tablespoons all-purpose flour
3 eggs
1/2 cup light cream *or* nonfat milk
2 tablespoons ground ginger
Pepper to taste
3 tablespoons minced crystallized ginger
Vegetable oil for frying

Grate sweet potatoes with a hand grater.
Place in the center of a clean cotton kitchen
towel and squeeze tightly to extract as much
liquid as possible. Transfer potatoes to a
large bowl. Add the scallions, gingersnap
crumbs and flour; toss to combine. Whisk
the eggs, cream, ground ginger and pepper.
Add to potato mixture and stir until well
blended. Stir in crystallized ginger.

Brush a large flat skillet with oil and heat
over medium-high heat. Using your hands,
shape potato mixture into small plump patties. Fry patties until crusty golden brown
on both sides.

mixed winter squash provençal

8 cups cubed peeled mixed winter squash
   (such as butternut, acorn and turban)
1/2 cup instant flour (such as Wondra)
2 teaspoons ground ginger
6 cloves garlic, minced
1/2 cup minced fresh parsley
2 tablespoons minced fresh rosemary
Salt and pepper to taste
1/3 cup plus 2 tablespoons olive oil, *divided*

Preheat oven to 325°. In a large bowl, toss
squash with flour and ginger. Stir in the
garlic, parsley and rosemary; season with
salt and pepper. Add 1/3 cup oil; toss to
coat. Transfer to a shallow 2-quart baking
dish. Drizzle with remaining oil. Cover and
bake for 1-1/2 hours. Uncover; bake 45-60
minutes longer or until the top is crusty
brown. (The long baking allows the bottom
layer of squash to almost melt while the top
layer forms an enticing crust.) Cool for a
few minutes before serving.

SERVES 8-12

pumpkin spice cake

3 cups sugar

1 cup shortening

3 eggs

1 can (15 ounces) pumpkin

3 cups all-purpose flour

2 teaspoons baking powder

1 teaspoon baking soda

1 teaspoon *each* ground cloves, nutmeg,
   cinnamon and allspice

1 teaspoon vanilla extract

brown sugar glaze:

1/2 cup packed brown sugar

2 tablespoons butter, melted and cooled

1 cup powdered sugar, sifted

1 tablespoon milk

Pecan halves for decoration

Preheat oven to 350°. With a mixer, cream sugar and shortening. Beat in eggs and pumpkin. Sift dry ingredients and add to creamed mixture. Add vanilla. Spoon into a greased and floured Bundt or tube pan. Bake for 1 hour or until a toothpick comes out clean. Cool for 30 minutes before removing from pan. For the glaze, stir brown sugar, butter, powdered sugar and milk until mixture is smooth (you might need a little more milk). Drizzle over cake; decorate with pecan halves.

SERVES 12-16

*Wine Recommendation for this menu: Australian unoaked
Chardonnay, dry Vouvray, Fumé or Sauvignon Blanc*

mama lucy's chicken baked in cream and lemon with rice

LUCY GOODRICH

1 fryer chicken, cut into pieces
Garlic salt and pepper
1 cup all-purpose flour
3 tablespoons peanut oil
3 cups cooked rice
1 large lemon, cut into 8 to 10 thin slices
Juice of 1 large lemon
1 pint half-and-half cream
1/2 pint heavy cream

Preheat oven to 375°. Season chicken pieces with garlic salt and pepper; season the flour with garlic salt and pepper. Dredge chicken in flour and shake off excess. Lightly brown in hot oil. (The point is to color it for looks and flavor, not to cook it, for it will cook in the oven.) Do not wash the sauté pan.

Place cooked rice in a lightly buttered baking dish; arrange chicken pieces on top. Place a lemon slice on each and sprinkle with lemon juice. In the sauté pan, bring half-and-half and heavy cream to a simmer; stir and scrape up any browned bits from the bottom of the pan. When cream begins to thicken, pour it over chicken and rice. Cover loosely with foil. Bake for 30 minutes. Remove foil and reduce heat to 325°. Bake for 15 more minutes.

SERVES 4-6

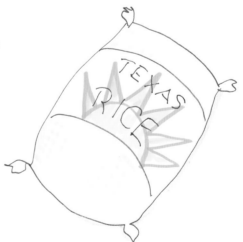

chicken with artichokes and fingerling potatoes

KATHY LOVE

3 thick slices of bacon, cut into pieces

1/4 cup olive oil

3 tablespoons all-purpose flour

1 teaspoon salt

1 teaspoon pepper

1 large package chicken thighs
(about 10 thighs)

2 cloves garlic, minced

2 tablespoons chopped fresh sage

2 teaspoons chopped fresh rosemary

1/2 cup white wine

2 cups chicken broth

2 tablespoons Cholula hot sauce

2 tablespoons Dijon mustard

30 small fingerling *or* new potatoes,
cut up to make 3-1/2 cups

2 packages (8 ounces *each*) frozen
artichoke hearts

Preheat oven to 350°. Cook bacon in a Dutch oven and remove when crispy. Add oil to drippings. Combine the flour, salt and pepper in a plastic bag; add chicken thighs, a few at a time, and shake to coat. Brown chicken in oil and drippings, removing pieces to a plate when browned. Add garlic and cook for a few minutes. Add sage and rosemary. Stir in wine and then the broth, hot sauce and mustard. Return chicken and bacon to the pan. Add potatoes and artichoke hearts. Cover and bake for 1 hour and 20 minutes.

SERVES 5-6

chicken, quick and easy

MARJORIE CRAWFORD

Sounds like a strange dish, but my kids love it!

4 boneless skinless chicken breast halves

1/2 cup Dijon mustard

1/4 cup teriyaki sauce

1/4 cup crumbled cooked bacon

1/2 cup grated Parmesan cheese

Preheat oven to 400°. Place chicken in a 13-inch x 9-inch x 2-inch glass baking dish. Spread mustard over chicken; pour teriyaki sauce evenly over the top. Sprinkle with bacon and cheese. Bake for 30 minutes.

SERVES 4

cranberry corn muffins

MIMI KERR

Our cornbread is a refinement of pone, which is bread made in the Colonial days from Indian meal (cornmeal).

I cup cornmeal
I cup all-purpose flour
2 tablespoons sugar
I tablespoon baking powder
I-I/2 teaspoons salt
I egg, beaten
I cup milk
I/2 cup butter, melted
I cup canned whole-berry cranberry sauce

Preheat oven to 400°. Lightly coat miniature muffin tins with nonstick cooking spray or use paper liners. In a large bowl, whisk the cornmeal, flour, sugar, baking powder and salt until well combined. Add egg, milk and butter, mixing with a large spoon until blended (do not overmix). Stir in cranberry sauce (you do not need to stir it very much). Spoon into muffin tins, filling each cup two-thirds full. Bake for 15 minutes or until a tester inserted in the center comes out clean.

MAKES I DOZEN

mixed grain salad with dried fruit

MARGARET GRIFFITH

I/4 cup vegetable oil
I/2 cup chopped shallots
I cup uncooked brown rice
I cup uncooked wild rice
I cup wheat berries
2 cups water
2 cups chicken stock
3/4 cup dried cranberries
I/2 cup chopped dried apricots
I/2 cup dried currants
I/2 cup sherry wine vinegar
2 tablespoons walnut oil *or* olive oil
2 tablespoons chopped fresh sage*
Salt and pepper to taste
I cup coarsely chopped pecans

Heat the oil in a large saucepan over medium-high heat. Add shallots and sauté until translucent, about 5 minutes. Add brown rice, wild rice and wheat berries; stir to coat. Add water and stock. Bring to a boil and then reduce heat to low. Cover and cook for 40 minutes or until rice is tender. Remove from the heat and stir in the fruit. Cool to room temperature.

In a small bowl, whisk the vinegar, oil and sage. Pour over salad and toss to coat. Season with salt and pepper. This can be prepared a day ahead, covered and refrigerated. Bring to room temperature before serving. Stir in the pecans just before serving.

I usually use lots more than 2 tablespoons of sage. You can use 2 teaspoons dried sage if you must.

carrot pudding
FRANCITA ULMER

4 pounds carrots, sliced
6 eggs, *separated*
1 cup sugar
12 ounces rice flour
12 ounces unsalted butter, melted and cooled
1/2 pound cheddar cheese, shredded
1-1/2 teaspoons salt
1 tablespoon baking powder

Preheat oven to 500° (don't forget to lower heat later). Place a baking sheet in oven. Cook carrots until very soft; drain and purée in a food processor. In a mixing bowl, beat egg yolks until thick. Add sugar and beat until well incorporated. Beat in flour alternately with melted butter. Stir in carrot purée, cheese and salt. Add baking powder last. Beat egg whites until stiff; fold into carrot mixture.

Spoon into a buttered 13-inch x 9-inch x 2-inch baking dish. Place dish on baking sheet. Bake for only 10 minutes. Then lower temperature to 350° and continue baking for 55 minutes. Check at 45 minutes. Pudding should be soft and spongy to the touch and browned on top, but moist inside.

SERVES 12

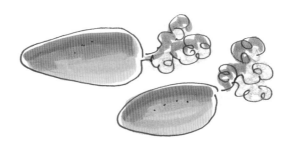

apple cranberry cobbler with sugar cookie crust

MIMI KERR

filling:

9 Granny Smith, Fuji *or* Gala apples,
   cored and diced
1 cup chopped dried cranberries, optional
Zest of 1 lemon
Juice of 1/2 lemon
1/2 cup sugar
1/4 cup packed brown sugar
1/2 teaspoon ground cinnamon

crust:

1 cup unsalted butter, softened
1 cup sugar
1 egg
1-1/2 cups all-purpose flour
1 teaspoon baking powder
1/4 teaspoon salt
1 teaspoon vanilla extract

Preheat oven to 350°. Toss apples and cranberries if desired with lemon zest, juice, sugars and cinnamon. Place in a 13-inch x 9-inch x 2-inch baking dish. In a large mixing bowl, cream butter, sugar and egg. Combine the flour, baking powder and salt; add to creamed mixture along with vanilla. Stir to combine.

Using a spoon, drop large dollops of batter over the apples, leaving spaces in between. Bake for 40 minutes or until golden brown. Delicious served with whipped cream or cinnamon ice cream.

SERVES 12

wondrous winter

wondrous Winter

The weather may turn chilly at this time of year, but our homes are filled with warmth! There's the magic of Christmas, with gifts from the kitchen (and from Santa) and family gatherings, always involving food…ringing in the New Year with celebratory drinks and hors d'oeuvres…hosting football-watching parties for college bowl games and the Super Bowl…and making sweets or a special meal for your Valentine.

Texans celebrate rodeos and stock shows that circulate throughout the state this time of year. And now's the season for making soups, stews and other hearty winter favorites. We've even included recipes and tips for observing Chinese New Year…seafood specialties to mark Mardi Gras…an appropriate Presidents' Day dessert…Irish dishes for St. Patrick's Day…and fun foods for Oscar Night.

During the winter, we decorate our homes and entertain often. The garden is taking a bit of time off, but we plant our chilled spring bulbs and keep mulch on the flower beds; pine needles make the best mulch, and the pine branches are an ideal local resource for greenery for decoration. Garden Club members like to "be green," and we use local—and often free—decorations.

While taking the dog for a walk, it's fun to gather pinecones from the neighborhood streets. Pinecones are beautiful in baskets. Leave them natural, or add a festive touch by spraying with gold paint—either brushed lightly or turned "solid gold." Why not try silver spray paint to match the silverware on your holiday table? Masses of candles of all different heights look inviting even when they aren't lit.

During the winter, we decorate our homes and entertain often…the garden is taking a bit of time off.

Shiny red and green apples look great piled in a big bowl. Eat them later, or bake them into one of our delicious recipes. Bois d'arc apples, also known as Osage oranges, are hanging heavy on the trees. They repel pests and add a lush lime color with lots of texture. In a basket or bowl, they add a long-lasting and economical splash of color. Mix in pomegranates for a different take on the traditional red and green.

We have learned many tricks to keep our decorations fresh. Ivy and poinsettias can be watered, then placed in plastic bags and closed up tight; they will last nearly the whole season without being watered and can then be planted or put in a greenhouse later. Napkins or color- ful cloths can be tied to cover the bags. Mosses look gorgeous covering a table or mantel. Greens should be "spritzed" with water from a spray bottle so they don't dry out.

And then there are winter herbs for a bit of flavor. Cold-weather plants we like to use in cooking and in our arrangements are cilantro, dill, parsley, sorrel, garlic, fennel, nasturtium— colorful, edible and nutritious—arugula or rocket plant (a must for Italian dishes) and germander. Mexican mint marigold is Texas' answer to tarragon.

Enjoy the beautiful decorations from nature and many festive occasions of this season. Revel in the wonders of winter!

GIFTS FROM THE KITCHEN

At Christmastime, homemade and home-baked items make the most thoughtful and economical gifts. Recycle or buy attractive bottles, containers or jars to present your gift…festive ribbons or raffia tied around jars and bottles make them special. You can spray-paint bottles with gold or silver paint and add an attractive cork for a more impressive look; however, nothing is more beautiful than a bottle of beautiful herb vinegar.

tips for making herb vinegar

* Sterilize glass bottles (nothing metallic) in boiling water for 10 minutes.
* Pick the herbs fresh in the morning when the essential oils will be strongest. Wash them well and pat dry.
* Fill the bottle a fourth to half full with herbs. Cover completely with vinegar (heating the vinegar first will speed the process).
* Choose white vinegar for delicate herbs, red for stronger flavors such as garlic.
* Set aside for 2 to 4 weeks. Taste…if it's too strong, dilute with more vinegar.
* Strain out the old herbs and replace with new ones, just for looks.

hot mustard

KAY HEDGES

Homemade hot mustard is considered a must for our family at Christmas! It has been a tradition for several generations, as there is no better accompaniment to turkey and ham, alone or in sandwiches. It keeps a long time in the refrigerator (if there is any left) and goes well with a variety of different meats.

1 can (4 ounces) Coleman's dry mustard
1 cup cider vinegar
2 eggs
1 cup sugar
Dash of salt

Soak mustard in vinegar after mixing and stirring slowly. Let stand overnight. In a saucepan, whisk eggs; stir in the sugar, salt and mustard mixture. Cook and stir over medium heat until mixture thickens, which is usually at the boiling point. Let cool slightly; pour into jars and refrigerate.

MAKES 3 CUPS

honey pear conserve

KAREN TERRELL

An excellent side dish for a ham or turkey dinner.

4 pounds Anjou pears, peeled and
   cut into 1-inch pieces
1 cup honey (or to taste)
3/4 cup lemon juice
2 teaspoons ground cinnamon
1/2 teaspoon ground cloves
1/2 cup dried currants

In a large saucepan, combine the pears, honey, lemon juice, cinnamon and cloves. Cook and stir over medium heat until the liquid begins to simmer. Reduce heat and simmer for 35-45 minutes or until thickened, stirring occasionally. Add the currants; simmer, partially covered, for 15 more minutes. Transfer to a bowl; let it cool. Cover and chill overnight or for up to 1 week.

limoncello

DELBY WILLINGHAM

Making homemade citron vodka is a snap...clean and peel the zest of one or two citrons, place in a clean bottle and cover with grain alcohol. You can use the zest several times, if you leave it in the bottle. After adding vodka, rest a month before using.

2 pounds lemons
4 cups 100-proof vodka
3 cups sugar
3 cups water

Peel lemons and put peels only (not the white pith) in a large bowl; cover with vodka. Let stand at room temperature for 1 week.

In a large saucepan over medium heat, stir sugar and water until the sugar dissolves; cool. Add to the vodka mixture and stir. Strain and pour the liquid into bottles. Seal and chill for at least 1 month. Pour into pretty bottles with corks for Christmas presents. Add a strip of lemon peel in the bottle for looks.

homemade vanilla extract

16 ounces vodka
2 ounces dark rum *or* brandy
6 vanilla beans (sold online)

Pour vodka and rum into a mason jar or bottle. Split vanilla beans in half, leaving 1 inch at the top. Stuff the beans in the jar and lock the lid tightly. Store in a dark pantry for at least 2 months, after which it will be ready to use.

HOMEMADE BROWN SUGAR COMES IN HANDY

It's easy to make homemade brown sugar: In a bowl, mix 1 cup sugar and 1 teaspoon molasses with a fork until well blended. Store in a ziplock bag. This recipe comes in handy when you run out of brown sugar and are in the middle of baking! It's also nice to tie up a little bag to go with your gift cookies!

amy's chocolate brownie pie

DANA PARKEY

*I use a foil pan so it will be ready to give as a gift. After the
pie is cooled, I place a paper doily on top and wrap with
cellophane.*

2 eggs
1 cup sugar
1/2 cup butter, melted
1/2 cup all-purpose flour
1/3 cup baking cocoa
1/4 teaspoon salt
1/2 cup semisweet chocolate chips
1 teaspoon vanilla extract
1/2 cup chopped nuts, optional

Preheat oven to 350°. In a mixing bowl, mix
eggs, sugar and butter. Stir in flour, cocoa and
salt, beating until blended. Stir in chocolate
chips, vanilla and nuts if desired. Spread into
a greased 8-inch pie pan. Bake for 35 minutes
or until set.

Serves 6–8

CHRISTMAS

Christmas is, of course, special. We have gathered a special Christmas Eve menu along with our best for the big day itself—from an easy breakfast dish to a variety of side dishes and desserts for your family's feast.

green salad

2 large bunches of spinach
1 large Granny Smith green apple, chopped
1 cup pecans, roasted
Chopped red onion to taste
Dried cranberries to taste

dressing:

1 tablespoon sugar
2/3 cup vegetable oil
6 tablespoons spicy mango ginger chutney
3 tablespoons lemon juice
1 teaspoon curry powder
1 teaspoon dry mustard
1/2 teaspoon salt

In a salad bowl, combine the spinach, apple, pecans, onion and cranberries. In a small bowl, whisk the dressing ingredients until blended. Drizzle over salad and toss to coat.

Christmas Eve Dinner ~ Susan Miclette

When my brother was sent to Vietnam before Christmas of 1966, my parents wanted to change the way we did Christmas while he was gone. We started having a Christmas Eve dinner, then a Christmas brunch after opening presents and then eating left-overs on Christmas evening. The tradition stuck.

Our typical Christmas Eve dinner includes: Green Salad, Best Prime Rib, Yorkshire Pudding, Merry Berry Salad, fresh green beans with almond slivers and Pumpkin Roll for dessert. The Green Salad has varied over the years; the most recent one is my favorite. I believe the prime rib recipe was included in the first Junior League of Houston Cookbook.

best prime rib

1 prime rib roast (3 to 4 ribs, 6 to 8 pounds)
Salt and pepper

At noon, preheat the oven to 375°. Season
the roast with salt and pepper; let the meat
get to room temperature before roasting.
Roast for 45 minutes. Turn the oven off and
do not open the oven. Forty minutes before
serving, turn the oven on again to 375°.
Roast will be medium-rare in center and
well-done around the edges. We usually do
this early afternoon and don't eat it until
7:30 or 8. It works great if you are going to
church or a holiday party and don't have
anyone watching your dinner.

yorkshire pudding

6 tablespoons drippings from roast
   prime rib*
2 eggs, room temperature
1 cup milk, room temperature
1 cup sifted flour
1/2 teaspoon salt

Add enough drippings to muffin pan and
heat to 450°. In a mixing bowl, beat eggs
until light. Beat in milk until frothy. Add
flour and salt; beat until smooth. Fill muffin
cups half full. Bake for 15 minutes. Reduce
the temperature to 350°; bake 15 minutes
more. Do not open the oven until done.
Serve immediately with butter.

*If you don't have sufficient beef drippings, get extra beef fat
from the butcher and cook it separately.*

MAKES 8 MUFFINS (I USUALLY TRIPLE
THIS FOR 8-10 PEOPLE)

merry berry salad

1 package (6 ounces) raspberry gelatin
2-1/2 cups boiling water, *divided*
3 packages (10 ounces *each*) frozen raspberries
1 teaspoon lemon juice
1 cup (8 ounces) light sour cream
1 package (6 ounces) cherry gelatin
1 can (20 ounces) crushed pineapple
1 can (16 ounces) whole-berry cranberry sauce

Dissolve raspberry gelatin in 1-1/2 cups boiling water. Add frozen raspberries and lemon
juice, stirring until thawed. Pour into a
13-inch x 9-inch x 2-inch pan. Refrigerate
until firm. Cover with sour cream. Dissolve
cherry gelatin in remaining boiling water;
add pineapple and cranberry sauce. Chill
until slightly thickened. Pour over sour
cream layer. Chill thoroughly.

SERVES 15-18

pumpkin roll

3/4 cup all-purpose flour
2 teaspoons ground cinnamon
1-1/2 teaspoons ground ginger
1 teaspoon ground nutmeg
1 teaspoon baking powder
1/2 teaspoon salt
3 eggs
1 cup sugar
2/3 cup canned pumpkin
1 teaspoon lemon juice
Powdered sugar for towel and dusting

filling:

1 package (8 ounces) cream cheese, softened
1/4 cup butter, softened
1 cup powdered sugar
1 teaspoon vanilla extract

Preheat oven to 350°. Grease, flour and line a jelly-roll pan with waxed paper. Sift dry ingredients together and set aside. With a mixer, beat eggs on high speed for 1-2 minutes. Add sugar slowly. Beat for a total of 5 minutes. Stir in pumpkin and lemon juice. Fold in dry ingredients. Spread into prepared pan. Bake for 12 minutes or until cake is springy to the touch. Sprinkle a tea towel with powdered sugar. Turn out cake onto towel; remove waxed paper. Roll up and refrigerate for 3 hours.

With a mixer, beat the filling ingredients until smooth. Unroll cake and spread with filling. Roll up again; dust with powdered sugar.

Wine Recommendation for this menu: Sister Creek Vineyards Cabernet Sauvignon

Go through your Christmas cards and save the beautiful ones for decoupage...or clip off the fronts to make next year's packages prettier.

make-ahead christmas morning french toast soufflé

JUNE STOBAUGH

8 slices sturdy white bread (such as
   Pepperidge Farm Hearty White), cubed
1 package (8 ounces) cream cheese, softened
9 eggs
1-1/2 cups milk
2/3 cup half-and-half cream
1/2 cup maple syrup
1/2 teaspoon vanilla extract
Ground cinnamon
Powdered sugar
Additional maple syrup, warmed

Place bread cubes in a buttered 13-inch x
9-inch x 2-inch baking dish. With a mixer,
beat cream cheese on medium speed until
smooth. Add eggs, one at a time, mixing well
after each addition. Add milk, half-and-half,
syrup and vanilla; mix until smooth. Pour
over bread. Cover and refrigerate overnight.

Remove from the refrigerator 30 minutes
before baking. Preheat oven to 375°.
Uncover baking dish; sprinkle cinnamon
over the top. Bake for 50 minutes or until
set. Sprinkle with powdered sugar; serve
with warm syrup.

12 SERVINGS

christmas fruit salad

GAIL ORR

We eat this red and green salad for brunch on Christmas morning with smoked turkey and cheese grits. If you don't have time to make the cherry vinegar dressing, serve with poppy seed dressing.

Rosemary topiaries go on sale after Christmas. Keep it pruned in the cone shape and you'll not only enjoy a delightful garden accent but you'll have fresh rosemary to use in cooking.

Watermelon and honeydew, sliced and
    cut into bite-size pieces
Green grapes, sliced in half
Kiwi, sliced or cut into bite-size pieces
Dried cherries *or* cranberries

cherry vinegar dressing:

3/4 cup cherry vinegar
1/2 cup water
6 tablespoons sugar
1 teaspoon salt
6 tablespoons finely chopped fresh mint

Arrange the fruit on a serving platter or toss in a bowl; set aside. In a microwave-safe bowl, combine the vinegar, water, sugar and salt. Microwave on high for 3 minutes; whisk well to make sure the sugar is dissolved. Add mint; cool. Drizzle dressing over fruit, toss with the fruit or serve on the side.

MAKES 1-3/4 CUPS DRESSING

cranberry jewels

RUBY MONDAY

This simple recipe produces beautiful, translucent cranberries for a relish, salad or garnish. You may make it ahead of time, as it keeps well. And since you use a plastic bag to toss the berries and foil for baking them, there's no cleanup!

1 pound fresh cranberries, picked over
1 cup sugar

Preheat oven to 350°. Wash cranberries; place while still wet in a quart bag. Add sugar and mix well. Pour onto a large sheet of foil. Place a second sheet of foil on top to completely cover; crimp the two sheets together. Place on a jelly-roll pan. Bake for 1 hour.

SERVES 12-16

A Thanksgiving and Christmas tradition when I was growing up in Pittsburgh was to have orange sherbet in place of salad. I have no idea how it got started, and never thought to ask Mom! But it's terrific, and now all the kids insist on it. This is a great palate cleanser and foil for the rich food. ~Delby Willingham

hot curried fruit

MARY LOU SWIFT

This is a versatile recipe—serve over vanilla ice cream or as a separate dessert, or even as a side dish to ham or beef.

1 can (29 ounces) apricot halves, drained
1 can (29 ounces) pear halves, drained
1 can (29 ounces) peach halves, drained
1 can (20 ounces) pineapple chunks, drained
3/4 cup golden raisins
1/2 cup butter
1/2 cup packed brown sugar
1 teaspoon curry powder*
3/4 cup bourbon
1 cup heavy cream

Preheat oven to 400°. In a 2-1/2-quart casserole, combine the fruit and raisins. Melt butter in a small saucepan; stir in brown sugar and curry powder. Cook and stir over low heat until sugar is dissolved. Pour over fruit mixture; mix gently. Add bourbon. Cover and bake for 30 minutes or until heated through. Add heavy cream before serving.

* I actually add more than that to make certain the contrast of the sweet/curry taste is created.

SERVES 10-12

spinach madeleine

BARBARA KRAFT

I like to make this side dish the day before, since the flavor improves as it sits overnight. This can also be frozen.

2 packages (10 ounces *each*) frozen
  chopped spinach
1/4 cup butter
2 tablespoons all-purpose flour
2 tablespoons chopped onion
1/2 cup evaporated milk
1 teaspoon Worcestershire sauce
1 teaspoon celery salt
1 teaspoon garlic salt
1 teaspoon pepper
Salt and red pepper to taste
8 ounces Velveeta cheese, cubed
Buttered bread crumbs

Cook spinach according to package directions; drain and reserve cooking liquid. Set spinach aside. Melt butter in a saucepan over low heat. Add flour, stirring until blended and smooth but not brown. Add onion; cook until soft but not brown. Slowly add milk and reserved spinach cooking liquid, stirring constantly to avoid lumps. Cook and stir until smooth and thick. Add Worcestershire sauce, seasonings and cheese; stir until melted. Combine with cooked spinach. Serve immediately, or transfer to a casserole and refrigerate overnight.

If making ahead, remove casserole from the refrigerator 30 minutes before baking. Preheat oven to 350°. Top with buttered bread crumbs. Bake, uncovered, for 30-45 minutes or until bubbly and lightly browned.

SERVES 5-6

horseradish mousse

ANNE WALES

2 envelopes (1/4 ounce *each*)
  unflavored gelatin
1/4 cup cold water
1 cup heavy cream *or* half-and-half
1 cup whole milk
1 jar (5 ounces) cream-style horseradish
2 to 3 drops Worcestershire sauce
1/4 teaspoon prepared mustard
Tabasco, salt and cayenne pepper to taste
1 cup heavy cream, whipped

Dissolve gelatin in cold water. In a saucepan, heat cream and milk; add gelatin and stir over low heat to dissolve completely. Add horseradish, Worcestershire sauce, mustard and seasonings. Chill until medium thick. Fold in whipped cream. Transfer to a greased mold. Chill until set. Unmold onto a serving platter; garnish as desired.

SERVES 8-10

cheese teasers

VERLINDE DOUBLEDAY

Good for nibbling while opening presents!

1 jar (8 ounces) Old English cheese spread
1/2 cup butter, softened
1-1/4 cups all-purpose flour
1/2 teaspoon cayenne pepper
Paprika and salt to taste

Mix cheese spread and butter; add flour and spices. Roll into a log about 1-1/2 inches in diameter; wrap in waxed paper. Refrigerate overnight or until very firm. Preheat oven to 300°. Slice log very thin onto a nonstick cookie sheet. Bake for 15-17 minutes. Cool on racks. Store in an airtight container.

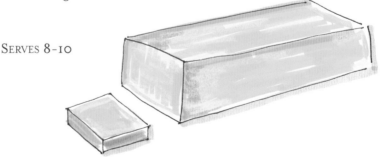

wassail

MARY LOU SWIFT

This recipe is easily doubled and can be served in a Wassail bowl or heatproof punch bowl.

1 quart apple cider
1/2 cup packed dark brown sugar
1/2 cup dark rum
1/2 cup brandy
1 tablespoon orange liqueur
   (Cointreau *or* Triple Sec)
1/4 teaspoon ground cinnamon
1/4 teaspoon ground cloves
1/8 teaspoon ground allspice
Dash salt
1/2 lemon and 1/2 orange, thinly sliced
Whipped cream
Freshly ground nutmeg

In a large saucepan over medium heat, bring cider to a boil. Add brown sugar; cook and stir until the sugar dissolves. Remove from the heat; stir in rum, brandy, liqueur, cinnamon, cloves, allspice and salt. Add lemon and orange slices. Heat the mixture over medium heat, stirring for 2 minutes. Ladle into mugs or wineglasses; top with a dollop of whipped cream and a sprinkle of nutmeg.

SERVES 6

cream cheese pound cake

KELLI CRAVENS

This is a simply delicious dessert to serve after a big feast. It also tastes wonderful toasted on Christmas morning!

1-1/2 cups butter, room temperature
1 package (8 ounces) cream cheese,
   room temperature
3 cups sugar
6 eggs, room temperature
3 cups all-purpose flour
1 teaspoon vanilla extract

Preheat oven to 325°. In a mixing bowl, beat butter and cream cheese until smooth and uniform in color. Gradually add sugar, beating until light and fluffy. Add eggs, one at a time, beating well after each addition. Beat in flour and vanilla until blended. Spoon into a greased and floured tube pan. Bake for 1 hour and 20 minutes or until a toothpick comes out clean.

SERVES 12-16

NEW YEAR'S EVE & DAY

*New Year's Eve is a festive time for a gathering of friends to toast a new beginning.
On New Year's Day, serving black-eyed peas is a must for good luck. Our Old
South Brunch is ideal for parade and football game watching.*

avocado crab dip

DODIE JACKSON

1 large ripe avocado, peeled and pitted
1 tablespoon lemon juice
2 tablespoons grated yellow onion
1 teaspoon Worcestershire sauce
1 package (8 ounces) cream cheese, softened
1/2 cup sour cream
1/2 teaspoon salt
1/2 pound fresh lump crabmeat, flaked

In a bowl, mash the avocado; mix with lemon
juice, onion and Worcestershire sauce. Stir
in cream cheese, sour cream and salt. Add
crabmeat and mix thoroughly. Serve with
tortilla chips or crackers.

MAKES 2 CUPS

tangy crabmeat appetizer

MARJORIE CRAWFORD

1 medium sweet onion, diced
1/2 cup vegetable oil
1/3 cup cider vinegar
3/4 teaspoon salt
1/2 teaspoon pepper
Capers, optional
1 pound fresh lump crabmeat, flaked

In a bowl, mix the onion, oil, vinegar, salt, pepper and capers if desired. Gently add the crab and thoroughly combine. Cover and chill for 8 hours or more. To serve, place the mixture in a dish of ice and garnish with parsley. Serve with crackers.

black bean cheese dip

MIMI KERR

1 pound bulk sausage
2 large cloves garlic, minced
3 cans (15 ounces *each*) black beans, rinsed and drained
3/4 cup chicken broth
1-1/2 teaspoons chili powder
1-1/2 teaspoons salt
6 to 10 drops Tabasco
8 ounces crumbled goat cheese
1 cup (4 ounces) shredded Monterey Jack cheese
3 tablespoons chopped fresh cilantro

In a large nonstick skillet, crumble and brown sausage; add garlic halfway through cooking. Do not wash pan. Place beans in the bowl of a food processor. Add sausage, broth, chili powder, salt and Tabasco. Process until beans are fairly smooth. Taste for seasoning. Return bean-sausage mixture to skillet the sausage was cooked in. Cook over medium-high heat for a few minutes, stirring well. Transfer to a shallow baking dish; sprinkle with cheeses. Can be refrigerated at this point until serving time.

At serving time, preheat oven to 300° and remove dip from the refrigerator. Bake for 25-30 minutes or until dip is bubbly around the sides, beans are heated through and the cheese is soft and creamy. Sprinkle with cilantro. Serve with tortilla chips.

SERVES A CROWD

cheese dip in french bread

BETTY DAVIS

This is quite attractive on the table. After the dip is gone from the bread, the "insides" of the bread with the cheese makes a delicious treat the next day.

2 cups (8 ounces) shredded sharp
   cheddar cheese
1-1/2 cups (12 ounces) sour cream
1 package (8 ounces) cream cheese, softened
Dash of Worcestershire sauce
1 jar dried beef, chopped and rinsed
1 bunch green onions, chopped
1 small round loaf of French bread
   (preferably a brioche), hollowed out

Preheat oven to 325°. Mix the first six ingredients together; pour into the hollowed-out loaf of bread. Wrap in foil. Bake for 1-1/2 hours. Serve with pita chips or toast points.

chicken liver pâté

JULIA HANCOCK

1 cup chicken stock
1/2 pound chicken breast, skin removed
1/2 pound chicken livers
1/4 cup chopped onion
1 clove garlic, crushed
4 hard-boiled eggs
2 tablespoons Dijon mustard
2 tablespoons lemon juice
1 teaspoon cognac
1 teaspoon dried rosemary, crushed
1 teaspoon salt
1/4 teaspoon pepper
1/4 teaspoon cayenne pepper
Pinch of ground cloves
3/4 cup butter, cubed

In a saucepan, bring stock to a simmer. Add chicken breast; cook gently below boiling point for 10 minutes. Meanwhile, prepare chicken livers by gently scraping them to remove the nerves. (This membranous part of the meat becomes tough when cooked and takes away from the smooth texture of the finished pâté.) Add liver to the saucepan; continue simmering the mixture for 5 minutes or until it almost loses its pinkness and the chicken breast meat is white and opaque. (If the liquid is allowed to boil, the meat will become tough and stringy. If it simmers too long, it will develop a grainy texture.)

Drain the meat through a sieve and reserve the liquid. Although the chicken stock is now discolored by the meat, it can be reserved for soups, or it can be clarified and used to make an aspic coating for the pâté. Allow the meat to stand about 5 minutes to cool and continue to drain.

Place the meat, onion and garlic in a food processor; blend for 1 minute or until smooth. Add eggs, mustard, lemon juice, cognac, rosemary, salt, pepper, cayenne and cloves; blend again until perfectly smooth. Now add the butter bit by bit while continuing to process. (The addition of butter makes the pâté smooth and creamy. If it is added while the meat is still hot, it will melt and then cool to a hard consistency.) Taste for seasoning. Pâté should be somewhat overseasoned because as it chills, the seasonings lose their strength.

Pack the mixture into a terrine. Garnish the top with chopped fresh parsley, slices of truffle and/or chopped hard-boiled egg yolk. Or the pâté mixture can be chilled until firm, then shaped into a ball or log and rolled in chopped parsley, pistachios or cayenne pepper.

SERVES 10-12

Wine Recommendation: Messina Hof Paulo Port

black-eyed pea dip

DELBY WILLINGHAM

2 cans (15 ounces *each*) black-eyed peas,
   rinsed and drained
5 fresh *or* canned jalapeños, chopped*
1/3 cup chopped onion
1 clove garlic
1 cup butter, cubed
2 cups (8 ounces) shredded sharp processed
   American cheese
1 can (4 ounces) chopped green chiles

In a food processor, blend the peas,
jalapeños, onion and garlic until smooth.
Combine butter and cheese in the top
of a double boiler; bring water to a boil.
Reduce heat to low; cook, stirring often,
until melted. Add chiles and pea mixture;
stir well. Add more jalapeño seeds or liquid
(or Tabasco) if you like it hotter. Serve
warm with corn chips (such as Fritos Scoops).

* *If using fresh jalapeños, save some of the seeds. If using
canned, save 1–2 tablespoons of the liquid.*

MAKES ABOUT 6 CUPS

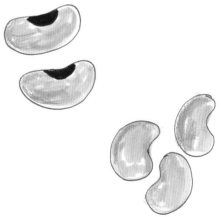

chocolate puddings with white brandy sauce

MARGARET GRIFFITH

1/2 cup milk

1/4 cup heavy cream

1 vanilla bean (3 inches), split lengthwise

4 squares (1 ounce *each*) unsweetened
   chocolate, finely chopped

6 tablespoons unsalted butter, softened

1-1/4 cups sugar, *divided*

4 eggs, *separated*

1/2 cup all-purpose flour

1/8 teaspoon cream of tartar

sauce:

2 cups finely chopped white chocolate

1 cup heavy cream

1 ounce brandy (or more)

Preheat oven to 350°. Butter the bottoms
of 8 ramekins (line ramekins with buttered
parchment paper if planning to remove to
serve). Scald milk, cream and vanilla bean
over medium heat and then strain into a
small bowl. Add unsweetened chocolate; stir
until melted and smooth. Cool completely.

Using a mixer, cream butter. Gradually add
1 cup sugar, continuing to beat until light.
Beat in the egg yolks, one at a time. Stir in
the chocolate mixture. Sift flour over mixture and stir to combine; set aside. Using
clean dry beaters, beat egg whites with cream
of tartar until soft peaks form. Gradually
beat in remaining sugar until stiff but not
dry. Fold a third of the egg whites into
chocolate mixture and then gently fold in
the rest. Divide among prepared ramekins.
Place in a large baking pan; add enough
water to pan so it comes halfway up the sides
of ramekins. Bake for 50 minutes. Cool.
Refrigerate until chilled.

Make the sauce shortly before serving.
Place white chocolate in a bowl. In a
saucepan, bring cream to a boil, watching
carefully so it doesn't boil over. Pour
hot cream over chocolate and stir with a
wooden spoon until melted. Add brandy
and continue stirring until incorporated.
Pour over chilled puddings.

SERVES 8

undesignated driver's delight

FRANCEY PENGRA

This drink is best served after a light meal and with a designated driver!

6 tablespoons rum
6 tablespoons malted milk powder
6 tablespoons Kahlúa
6 scoops of chocolate ice cream
6 pinches ground bittersweet chocolate
Seltzer water
Espresso beans ground up to form powder

Pour rum, malted milk powder and Kahlúa into a blender and blend. Add ice cream and bittersweet chocolate; blend again. Pour into tall glasses (decorative, if you have them). Pour a small amount of seltzer water on top of each; sprinkle with ground espresso beans.

SERVES 6

new year's morning cheese danish

GAIL HENDRYX

1 package (8 ounces) cream cheese, softened
1/2 cup sugar
1 egg, *separated*
1 teaspoon vanilla extract
2 cans (8 ounces *each*) refrigerated
   crescent rolls

Preheat oven to 350°. Mix the cream cheese, sugar, egg yolk and vanilla. On a greased cookie sheet, roll out one can of rolls; press seams and perforations to seal. Spread cream cheese mixture over dough. Press out remaining can of rolls on top of filling; seal edges with fingertips. Whip egg white; brush over top of dough. Bake for 20 minutes.

SERVES 6

OLD SOUTH BRUNCH

We have shamelessly copied the idea and menu for this New Year's Day brunch and Bowl watching party from friends who host this party every two years. We have adapted our own recipes and added a few to the festivities. The hostess always decorates her table with amaryllis bought at the Bulb Mart and forced into bloom for just that day. Her name is protected for obvious reasons, as she cannot invite all of our dear readers, as much as she would love to.

The menu features: Screwy Marys for a Crowd, Salty Hair of the Dog, Olive Cheese Balls, Jezebel Sauce with Ham, Black-Eyed Peas, Slow-Baked Tomatoes, biscuits (purchased or homemade), cheese grits (see recipe on page 247 but omit the shrimp), Mom's Best Brownies, and salty nuts and assorted cookies (purchased or homemade).

screwy mary

The twist is the addition of orange juice; this recipe is used in Continental President's Clubs.

1 teaspoon orange juice
1/2 teaspoon lime juice
Dash of Tabasco
2 to 4 dashes of Worcestershire sauce
Pinch of prepared horseradish
1-1/2 ounces vodka
Mr. & Mrs. T Bloody Mary Mix *or*
    V-8 juice (enough to fill glass)
Lawry's Seasoned Salt to taste

Combine all ingredients in shaker; give a brisk shake and pour over ice in a highball glass. Adjust salt and "heat" to taste. To garnish, place a lime wedge on the rim of the glass or place a celery rib (with leaves) in the glass.

screwy marys for a crowd

1-1/2 bottles of Mr. & Mrs. T Bloody Mary
    Mix *or* 48 ounces V-8 juice
3/4 cup orange juice
3 tablespoons Worcestershire sauce
2 tablespoons prepared horseradish
2 tablespoons lime juice
1 teaspoon Tabasco
1 cup vodka

Combine all ingredients in a large pitcher (may need to mix up in batches); stir well. Pour over ice in highball glasses. Adjust salt and "heat" to taste. To garnish, place a lime wedge on the rim of the glass or place a celery rib (with leaves) in the glass.

SERVES 20

salty hair of the dog

1-1/2 ounces vodka
Freshly squeezed Ruby Red grapefruit juice
  (preferably Texas Valley)
Pinch of salt

Combine ingredients. Stir together or
shake in a cocktail shaker and pour over ice.
Garnish with a mint sprig or a thin grapefruit curl, carefully peeled with no pith.

olive cheese balls

MARIANNE CRAIN

1 jar (5 ounces) Old English cheese spread
1-1/2 cups all-purpose flour
1/2 cup butter, softened
Dash of salt and paprika
1 jar pimiento-stuffed olives, drained

Mix the cheese spread, flour, butter, salt
and paprika until well blended. Form balls
around olives. Refrigerate or freeze until
ready to use. Bake at 350° until browned.
If frozen, bake at 450°.

jezebel sauce

GAY ESTES

A spicy and pungent sauce for ham or canapés.

1 jar (10 ounces) apple jelly
1 jar (10 ounces) pineapple *or*
  apricot preserves
3/4 cup prepared horseradish
1 tablespoon dry mustard
1/2 teaspoon lemon juice
Cracked fresh pepper

Combine all ingredients in a saucepan over
medium heat, stirring well until blended.
Cool and refrigerate overnight. Will keep
for weeks in the refrigerator.

black-eyed peas

GAY ESTES

An old Southern tradition for good luck coming.
Foreigners call these "cowpeas."

I pound dried black-eyed peas,
  soaked overnight
1/2 pound smoked bacon *or* ham hock
I large onion, sliced
I to 2 dashes Tabasco
I small jalapeño, seeded and sliced, optional
I clove garlic, minced, optional
I teaspoon sugar
I teaspoon salt

Place the soaked beans in a large pot. Add
the remaining ingredients. Bring to a boil;
reduce heat. Simmer for I to I-1/2 hours or
until beans are tender, stirring occasionally.

SERVES IO

slow-baked tomatoes

VIRGINIA WATT

3 medium tomatoes
6 cloves garlic, chopped
6 sprigs fresh thyme
3 tablespoons olive oil
Kosher salt and pepper to taste

Heat oven to 300°. Slice tomatoes in half
and squeeze out seeds. Place cut side up in
a baking dish. Scatter garlic and thyme over
the top. Drizzle with oil; season with salt and
pepper. Bake until tomatoes are soft but hold
their shape, about 2 hours.

SERVES 6

mom's best brownies

BROWNY BAKER

2 egg whites
I egg
3/4 cup sugar
6 tablespoons unsweetened applesauce
2 tablespoons vegetable oil
I-I/2 teaspoons vanilla extract
I/2 cup cake flour, sifted
I/2 cup baking cocoa
I/4 teaspoon salt
I tablespoon chopped walnuts, optional

Preheat oven to 350°. In a mixing bowl,
whisk the egg whites, egg, sugar, applesauce,
oil and vanilla. Combine the flour, cocoa
and salt; stir into egg mixture just until
blended (do not overmix). Pour into a
greased 8-inch square baking pan. Sprinkle
with walnuts if desired. Bake for 25 minutes
or until just set and a toothpick inserted in
center comes out clean. Cool on a wire rack
for at least I5 minutes before cutting.

MAKES ABOUT I DOZEN

CHINESE NEW YEAR

Chinese New Year is a major event for hundreds of thousands of Asian-Americans in the United States and worldwide for those of Chinese descent. It's also called Lunar New Year, as it ushers in the lunar year. Like all seasonal feasts, it is predicated on moon phases—this one falling on the second full moon following the winter solstice. Celebrations start on a date between late January and mid-February and last up to 15 days, concluding with the next full moon. The 15th day of the New Year is called the Lantern Festival, which is celebrated at night with lantern displays and children carrying lanterns in a parade.

In the days leading up to the celebration, families give their homes a thorough cleaning, hoping to sweep away any bad fortunes and to greet incoming luck. The eve of Chinese New Year is carefully observed with a feast for the entire family. At midnight, the family lights firecrackers to ward off evil spirits, and all the doors and windows are opened to let go of the old year and welcome the new one. In China, it is a tradition to "present the New Year's rice" by placing a wooden bowl on the altar dedicated to the family ancestors; this is believed to bring good luck.

This is a great time of year to enjoy a party or try some Asian recipes, and Asian food markets stock many items appropriate for the occasion.

beef stir-fry with snow peas and scallions

MIMI KERR

Stir-frying dates back to the earliest days of Asian cooking. Families cooked in woks over small wood-burning stoves.

1 flank steak (1 pound)
4 teaspoons cornstarch, *divided*
5 tablespoons water, *divided*
4 tablespoons vegetable oil, *divided*
3 tablespoons soy sauce
2 teaspoons dry sherry, optional
1/2 pound snow peas
1 bunch green onions
2 tablespoons oyster sauce
1/2 teaspoon sesame oil
3 slices peeled fresh gingerroot
1/2 teaspoon salt
Red pepper flakes, optional

Cut flank steak lengthwise into 1-1/2-inch-wide strips, then cut across the grain into 1/8-inch slices. For marinade, in a large bowl, combine 3 teaspoons cornstarch, 1 tablespoon water, 1 tablespoon vegetable oil, soy sauce and sherry if desired. Add beef slices and toss to coat thoroughly; let stand for 30 minutes.

Remove the tips and strings from snow peas; set aside. Cut green onion tops into 2-inch pieces and white portion into 1/4-inch pieces. In a small bowl, combine the remaining cornstarch and water until smooth. Stir in oyster sauce and sesame oil; set aside.

Heat the remaining vegetable oil in a wok over high heat. Add ginger; after a few seconds, add beef slices with marinade, onions and salt. Stir-fry for 2 minutes. Add peas and red pepper flakes if desired. Stir-fry 2-3 more minutes or until beef is cooked. Discard the ginger. Add cornstarch mixture to wok; stir until thickened.

SERVES 2-3

Wine Recommendation: Zinfandel, Grenache or Australian Shiraz

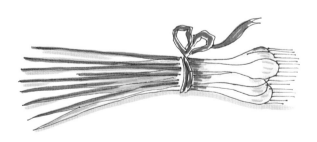

salmon with ginger and lemon

DELBY WILLINGHAM

To serve two, you can use the same amount of marinade for two salmon steaks. And when adding the sesame oil, go easy—it has a strong flavor!

4 salmon steaks *or* fillets
3 tablespoons soy sauce
1 tablespoon grated fresh
   gingerroot (or more)
1 teaspoon sesame oil
2 tablespoons chopped fresh cilantro
Grated zest and juice of 1 lemon

Place salmon pieces in a single layer in a glass baking dish. Combine the soy sauce, ginger and sesame oil; evenly pour over salmon. Cover and refrigerate for at least 30 minutes, but no more than 1 hour. Preheat oven to 350°. Bake salmon for 15 minutes or until fish flakes with a fork. Sprinkle with cilantro, lemon zest and juice.

SERVES 4

*Wine Recommendation: Chardonnay or
New Zealand Sauvignon Blanc*

traditional touches

- ଓ Red is the color for Chinese New Year and is thought to bring good luck, so decorate with red linens, dinnerware, candles and other items. Red envelopes with "good luck dollars" inside are a traditional gift for children and loved ones.
- ଓ Oranges and tangerines represent abundant happiness. Mandarin oranges, plentiful in China at the time of Chinese New Year, are another traditional gift. Have a bowl full of citrus for guests to enjoy.
- ଓ Plants and flowers symbolize rebirth and growth. Use fresh plant materials such as chrysanthemums, plum blossoms and bamboo.
- ଓ A circular tray symbolizes togetherness. Fill it with candies and goodies representing the sweetness of life. Eat a sweet so the year will be sweet!
- ଓ Serve Tsingtao Beer and Tiger Beer. The New Year's wishes are prosperity, longevity and health, and we can all drink to that!

sea bass with ginger and lime sauce
MARJORIE CRAWFORD

A delicious Asian-inspired fish dish.

2 tablespoons lime juice
1-1/2 tablespoons soy sauce
1 tablespoon chopped fresh cilantro
1 tablespoon chopped fresh gingerroot
1 tablespoon minced shallot
5 teaspoons olive oil, *divided*
Salt and pepper to taste
2 sea bass fillets (about 3/4 inch thick and 6 ounces *each*)

Preheat oven to 500°. In a small bowl, mix the lime juice, soy sauce, cilantro, ginger, shallot and 3 teaspoons oil. Season with salt and pepper. Brush a 9-inch glass dish with remaining oil. Place fish fillets in dish, turning to coat both sides with oil. Sprinkle fish with salt and pepper; spoon 1/2 tablespoon sauce over each fillet. Roast fish until just opaque in center, about 12 minutes. Top fish with remaining sauce.

SERVES 2

Wine Recommendation: for white, unoaked Chardonnay, Spanish Albarino, American or New Zealand Pinot Gris...for red, Messina Hof Reserve Pinot Noir

spicy sesame shrimp salad

CATHY PEARSON

dressing:

1/2 cup vegetable oil
1/2 cup sesame oil
1/3 cup red wine vinegar
1/3 cup soy sauce
3 tablespoons peanut butter
1/2 teaspoon crushed red pepper flakes
1/2 teaspoon ground ginger
I clove garlic, pressed

salad:

3/4 package farfalle (bow tie) pasta
I tablespoon vegetable oil
I clove garlic, pressed
I pound boiled shrimp
4 ounces sugar snap peas
4 to 6 green onions, chopped
1/3 cup fresh broccoli florets
I carrot, shredded
I-1/2 tablespoons sesame seeds, toasted

Place the dressing ingredients in a blender; blend thoroughly. Cook pasta according to package instructions; drain and place in a large bowl. Toss with oil and garlic. Add dressing while pasta is still warm; toss to coat. Cool. Add the rest of the salad ingredients; toss. Refrigerate for several hours or overnight.

SERVES 6-8

Wine Recommendation: Chablis, unoaked Chardonnay or Sancerre

the chinese zodiac

The Chinese use a 60-year lunar calendar, divided into five 12-year cycles, which dates back to 2600 B.C. Each of the 12 years is represented by an animal with different characteristics. A fun idea for a Chinese New Year theme party is to have a list of these animals and accompanying personality traits so guests can discern their particular sign, based on the year they were born. You can find more information at the library or online by searching "Chinese Zodiac."

SUPER BOWL

*When the "big game" rolls around in February, it's another great time to get together
and watch not only the football match, but the commercials too. Since everyone is
focused on the TV, dips and finger food are the perfect celebratory foods.*

spinach panini

KAY HEDGES

*This is a basic panini recipe, but any number of variations
are possible, limited only by your imagination. A panini
maker is desirable, but you can use a George Foreman
indoor grill, a waffle iron or just an ordinary skillet.*

4 slices (1/2 inch thick) crusty country-style
   bread (such as ciabatta or focaccia)
Olive oil
1 cup baby spinach
1/2 cup shredded *or* sliced mozzarella cheese
Roasted red pepper strips
Sliced prosciutto, turkey, ham *or*
   chicken, optional
Dried oregano

Brush one side of each bread slice with oil.
Lay two slices, oiled side down, and layer
with spinach, cheese, roasted peppers and
meat if desired. Sprinkle with oregano; top
with remaining bread, oiled side up. Press to
pack gently. Grill until bread is golden
brown and cheese is melted.

SERVES 2

artichoke pizza

MARY GRACE HAMILL

1 very thin 10-inch pizza crust
2 cups (8 ounces) shredded
   mozzarella cheese
1 cup canned water-packed
   artichokes, chopped
3 tablespoons capers
Olive oil
Minced fresh *or* dried oregano,
   salt and pepper to taste
Optional toppings: thinly sliced red
   onion, thinly sliced sun-dried
   tomatoes *and/or* halved kalamata olives

Preheat oven to 450°. Sprinkle pizza crust
with cheese, artichokes and capers; drizzle
with oil. Sprinkle with oregano, salt and
pepper. Top with onion, sun-dried tomatoes
and olives if desired. Bake for 10 minutes or
until crust is browned and cheese is melted.

collier's goat cheese appetizer

VERLINDE DOUBLEDAY

Olive oil
Cherry tomatoes, halved
Goat cheese log *or* round
Chopped *or* sliced fresh basil
Crackers

Preheat oven to 250°. Lightly grease a baking
sheet with oil. Place tomatoes, cut side down,
on oil. Bake until tomatoes start to collapse,
about 30 minutes. Place goat cheese in a
round glass pie plate; place in oven until
warmed. Toss basil with roasted tomatoes and
more oil; pour over heated cheese. Garnish
with more basil. Serve with crackers.

shrimp pâté

LIZ ROTAN

Fabulous on buttered toast or crackers or stirred into hot grits.

1 cup unsalted butter, cut into
   16 tablespoons, *divided*
1 pound fresh shrimp, peeled and deveined
1/2 teaspoon salt
1/2 teaspoon freshly ground pepper
1/4 cup sherry
2 tablespoons lemon juice
1/4 teaspoon cayenne pepper

Heat 6 tablespoons butter in a large skillet until hot and foaming. Add shrimp, salt and pepper; cook and stir over high heat for 4-7 minutes or until shrimp are pink and cooked through. Remove skillet from the heat; use a slotted spoon to transfer shrimp to a food processor fitted with a steel blade.

Return skillet to stove; add sherry, lemon juice and cayenne. Cook over high heat until liquid is reduced to approximately 3 tablespoons and is quite syrupy. Immediately add to shrimp in processor and process until shrimp are thoroughly puréed. With processor running, add remaining butter in pieces and process until thoroughly blended. Taste for seasoning, adding more salt, pepper, sherry, lemon juice or cayenne as needed. Transfer to a ceramic crock and cool completely. If not using right away, cover and refrigerate for up to 1 week. Bring to room temperature before serving.

MAKES 2-1/2 CUPS

bacon heaven

GAY ESTES

Wooden skewers
1-1/4 cups packed brown sugar (or a bit
   less to taste)
2 heaping teaspoons ground cinnamon
1 pound sliced bacon

Preheat oven to 350°. Soak skewers in cold water. In a shallow bowl, combine the brown sugar and cinnamon. Cut each bacon slice in half crosswise; dredge in cinnamon-sugar. Thread bacon on skewers, folding it like a ribbon. Place on foil you have "scrunched up" to prevent burning; place on a baking sheet or jelly-roll pan. Bake for 20 minutes or until crispy, not burned. Cool slightly before serving.

MAKES 32-36 BITES

spinach artichoke dip

LESLYE WEAVER

1 can (14 ounces) water-packed artichoke
    hearts, rinsed, drained and chopped
1 package (10 ounces) frozen chopped
    spinach, thawed and drained
1 cup grated Parmesan cheese
1 cup light mayonnaise
Sliced jalapeños to taste

Preheat oven to 350°. In a bowl, combine all
ingredients. Transfer to a greased shallow
baking dish. Bake for 20 minutes or until
bubbly. Serve with chips and vegetables.

february garden notes:

* Prune roses and repeat climbers.
* This is a great time to plant herbs
    such as cilantro, dill, fennel and sage.
* Plant citrus trees and shrubs now.
* Set out winter vegetables like cabbage
    and cauliflower.

VALENTINE'S DAY

For February 14, we serve up a menu of Cupid Soup (made with tomatoes, which were known as "love apples" in ancient times), a casserole of scalloped oysters and, of course, chocolate for dessert—your choice of three different cakes. For a beverage, we suggest Rose Champagne with a strawberry or cherry in the flute.

In addition to our menu, these foods are thought to be amatory—almonds, arugula, avocados, caviar, chili powder, eggs and honey.

If you plan to make a centerpiece, here is a tip: Red flowers zoom in cost at this time of year...roses, in fact, can cost up to three times the usual price. So why not choose pink or burgundy flowers instead and let your recipes speak to the theme? Now is the time to prune rosebushes, so bring the cut flowers in for a bouquet (sprinkle the table with petals if the roses are not pristine enough). And use red ribbons left over from Christmas to adorn the table.

breakfast for two

LYDIA HILLIARD

2 tablespoons butter
Chopped fresh mushrooms
Julienned cooked ham
Chopped green onions
Diced cooked potatoes
3 eggs
Water
Shredded cheddar cheese

Melt butter in an omelet pan. Sauté desired amounts of mushrooms, ham, green onions and potatoes. Beat eggs with a small amount of water; pour over ham and vegetables, stirring to mix. Sprinkle cheese on top as omelet begins to set. With a flip of the wrist, make a half moon of the omelet and serve on a heated plate.

tangy beets

MARGARET GRIFFITH

6 large beets, trimmed and peeled
1 small onion, minced
Salt and freshly ground pepper to taste
1/4 cup olive oil
1/4 cup cider vinegar
1 teaspoon Dijon mustard
1 teaspoon celery seed

Using a food processor fitted with a fine shredding disk, or a hand grater, finely grate beets. Transfer to a large bowl; add onion and combine well. Season with salt and pepper. In a small jar or bowl, combine remaining ingredients. Shake or whisk lightly to blend. Pour vinaigrette over beet mixture and toss to coat. Cover and refrigerate for several hours or up to 24 hours before serving.

SERVES 4

cupid soup

ANN WALES

2 cans (28 ounces *each*) whole
   tomatoes in juice
2 tablespoons brown sugar
5 shallots, finely diced
1 tablespoon tomato paste
Pinch of ground allspice
3 tablespoons butter *or* olive oil
2 tablespoons all-purpose flour
1-3/4 cups chicken broth
3 pieces thin white bread, crusts removed
2 tablespoons brandy *or* sherry, optional
1/4 teaspoon cayenne pepper
Sour cream for garnish

Preheat oven to 425°. Line a jelly-roll pan
or rimmed baking sheet with heavy-duty
foil. Drain tomatoes over a measuring cup;
squeeze out the excess juices, reserving all
juice. Place tomatoes on foil-lined pan;
sprinkle with brown sugar. Roast for 30
minutes or until tomatoes dry out and start
to caramelize. Cool slightly, then peel them
off the foil and set aside.

In a saucepan, sauté shallots with tomato
paste and allspice in butter until soft. Add
flour and cook for 1 minute to get rid of
the "floury" taste. Whisk in broth, then add
3 cups of reserved tomato liquid and the
roasted tomatoes. Bring to a boil. Reduce
heat; simmer for 10 minutes, adding bread
during the last 2 or 3 minutes. Purée the
soup in a blender; return to the saucepan.
Stir in brandy if desired and cayenne; heat
through. Garnish each bowl with a dollop
of sour cream.

SERVES 6–8

mama lucy's scalloped oysters

LUCY GOODRICH

A well-seasoned béchamel sauce and buttered cracker crumbs top a layer of oysters in this recipe. You'll need an ovenproof 2-quart serving dish, preferably shallow so there's a proper ratio between crispy topping and creamy oysters. Or you can prepare this in individual ramekins. Serve the oysters with chicken and rice, or in a shallow plate-rim bowl as a first course.

10 tablespoons unsalted butter, *divided*
5 green onions, finely chopped
3 to 4 large cloves garlic, minced
4 tablespoons all-purpose flour
2 cups 2% *or* whole milk
2 tablespoons Worcestershire sauce
2 tablespoons Tabasco
1 tablespoon lemon zest
1 teaspoon salt
1 teaspoon white pepper
1/4 teaspoon freshly grated nutmeg
1/4 teaspoon cayenne pepper
1 quart fresh oysters, well drained and
   liquor reserved
1 package very fresh crisp saltines, crushed
   (no dime-size pieces)

To make the béchamel sauce: In a 2-quart saucepan, melt 4 tablespoons butter; sauté green onions until soft. Add garlic; sauté 1 minute. Stir in flour and allow to cook but not color. Remove from the heat; whisk in milk until smooth. Return pan to stove and bring to a simmer; continue whisking, making sure to scrape the sides and bottom of pan. Stir in Worcestershire sauce, Tabasco, lemon zest, salt, pepper, nutmeg and cayenne. If sauce is very thick, add a little of the oyster liquor and simmer for a few minutes. Adjust seasoning; you can add more cayenne, but do not add so much as to be overpowering.

Preheat oven to 375°. Butter a 2-quart baking dish (with butter wrapper) and slip the oysters into it; dot with 2 tablespoons butter. Pour béchamel over oysters, spreading it to the edges. Bake, uncovered, for 20 minutes or until bubbly. Melt remaining butter; toss with saltine crumbs. Sprinkle over oysters. Bake until crackers are golden brown, about 10 minutes. Serve immediately.

SERVES 4–6

Wine Recommendation: Chardonnay or Champagne

beth's old-fashioned chocolate cake

KAREN TERRELL

2 cups all-purpose flour

2 teaspoons baking powder

2 teaspoons baking soda

1 teaspoon salt

2 cups sugar

2 cups water

4 squares (1 ounce *each*) unsweetened
chocolate, chopped

6 tablespoons unsalted butter, cubed

1 teaspoon vanilla extract

2 eggs, lightly beaten

chocolate frosting:

1-1/3 cups heavy cream

1-1/2 cups sugar

6 squares (1 ounce *each*) unsweetened
chocolate, chopped

10 tablespoons unsalted butter, cubed

1-1/2 teaspoons vanilla extract

Pinch of salt

Preheat oven to 350°. Butter and flour two 8-inch round cake pans; line with waxed paper. Sift together the flour, baking powder, baking soda and salt; set aside. In a saucepan, bring sugar and water to a boil, stirring until sugar dissolves. Pour into a large mixing bowl. Add chocolate and butter; let stand, stirring occasionally, until melted and slightly cooled. Stir in vanilla. Beat in the eggs at medium speed until combined. Add the dry ingredients all at once and beat until smooth. Divide batter evenly between prepared pans. Bake for 25 minutes or until a cake tester comes out clean. Cool in pans for 25 minutes, then invert onto a rack to cool completely.

To make the frosting: In a saucepan, bring cream and sugar to a boil over medium-high heat. Reduce heat; simmer, stirring occasionally, until the liquid reduces slightly, about 6 minutes. Pour into a medium bowl; add the chocolate, butter, vanilla and salt. Let stand, stirring occasionally, until chocolate and butter are melted. Set the bowl in a larger bowl of ice water. Using a handheld mixer, beat frosting on medium speed, scraping the sides occasionally with a rubber spatula, until thick and glossy, about 5 minutes. Use at once.

To assemble: Set one cake layer, right side down, on a serving platter. Using a metal spatula, spread a third of the frosting evenly over cake. Top with the second layer, right side up; frost top and sides with remaining frosting.

SERVES 12

molten chocolate babycakes

MARGARET PIERCE

4 eggs

Pinch of salt

1/4 cup unsalted butter, softened

3/4 cup superfine sugar

1 teaspoon vanilla extract

1/3 cup all-purpose flour

2 cups (12 ounces) high-quality bittersweet
or semisweet chocolate chips, melted
and cooled

Preheat oven to 400°. Grease a muffin tin
that makes 6 large muffins. In a mixing bowl,
beat eggs and salt until frothy; set aside.
Using an electric mixer, cream butter and
sugar. Gradually add egg mixture, then
vanilla, then flour, then chocolate, mixing
well with the addition of each ingredient.

Pour into muffin tin. Bake for 10 minutes,
removing from the oven while center is still
runny. Invert cakes onto dessert plates or
shallow bowls. Serve with a scoop of vanilla
ice cream and fresh raspberries on top. Or
serve with peppermint ice cream, topped
with crushed peppermint candies and
shaved chocolate.

SERVES 6

red velvet valentine cake

SCARLETT BALANTYNE

2-1/2 cups all-purpose flour
1-1/2 cups sugar
1 teaspoon baking soda
1 teaspoon salt
1 teaspoon baking cocoa
1-1/2 cups canola oil
1 cup buttermilk, room temperature
2 eggs, room temperature
2 tablespoons red food coloring
1 teaspoon white vinegar
1 teaspoon vanilla extract
Cream Cheese Frosting (recipe on page 34)
Valentine candies for decoration

Preheat the oven to 350°. Lightly grease and flour three 9-inch round cake pans; line with waxed paper. Sift together the flour, sugar, baking soda, salt and cocoa; set aside. In a large mixing bowl, whisk the oil, buttermilk, eggs, food coloring, vinegar and vanilla. Beat in the dry ingredients just until combined and a smooth batter is formed. Divide batter evenly among prepared pans. Place pans in the oven, evenly spaced apart. Bake for 30 minutes or until cake pulls away from sides of pans and a toothpick comes out clean. Rotate the pans halfway through baking time.

Remove cakes from the oven; run a knife around the edges to loosen from the pan. One at a time, invert the cakes onto a plate and then re-invert onto a cooling rack, rounded sides up. Frost when completely cool. Place the first layer round side down; spread with frosting. The second layer goes round side down. The third layer goes round side up! Decorate as desired.

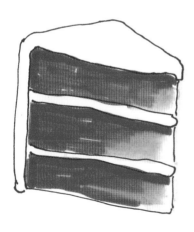

MARDI GRAS

Mardi Gras and Carnival are celebrated around the world as a time of feasting at the end of the Christmas season between January 6 (Day of Epiphany, Night of the Kings or Twelfth Night) and Shrove Tuesday, which precedes Lent and Ash Wednesday. Our thoughts turn to New Orleans, or Galveston, although others along the Gulf Coast lay claim to its beginnings, and Venice and Rio are well-known celebratory venues.

Carnival literally translates from Latin into "lose your flesh"—meaning party, party, party—and likely had its roots in pagan times. The season is one of parades, parties, balls (masked and otherwise), music, great food and beverages. Hospitality is a big part of the festivities, and gumbos, étouffées and other dishes feature the local bounty of seafood and shellfish.

We've compiled our favorite Cajun seafood recipes plus an appetizer and punch that would be perfect for a Mardi Gras party. Oysters and beignets are other good choices, and a King's Cake is a must (see page 141).

Jazz music is also a must. Beads in Mardi Gras colors—green for faith, gold for power and purple for justice—are easily obtained. And for a fun idea, have each guest make their own mask…provide paper plates, glue, tongue depressors, marking pins, scissors, yarn and feathers.

shrove tuesday pancakes

LYNN RAFFERTY

The idea is to eat all the butter and eggs—to use them up before the fasting season. The practice is so common that Shrove Tuesday is often referred to as Pancake Tuesday.

1 cup all-purpose flour
1 teaspoon baking soda
1 teaspoon sugar
1/2 teaspoon salt
1 pint buttermilk
2 eggs
2 tablespoons butter, melted

Mix dry and wet components in separate bowls, then stir together, leaving some lumps. Pour batter onto a lightly greased hot griddle. Turn when bubbles form on top; cook until second side is golden brown.

MAKES 16-18 PANCAKES

french 75 punch

DORIS HEARD

This drink was served at parties in New Orleans, where I grew up. I served it at a 1979 Christmas party in Friendswood, when the town was still recovering from 42 inches of rain from Tropical Storm Claudette. People still talk about the flood and the French 75 Punch. This is potent: Make sure there are designated drivers!

5 parts Champagne
1 part gin *or* brandy

Pour Champagne and gin into a punch bowl; add an ice ring to keep it cold. You can serve in glass Champagne flutes with a strawberry, cherry or lemon slice.

Variation: Substitute vodka for the gin; add a little lemon juice or sugar.

wallice durbin's hanky-panky

DORIS HEARD

My mother loved to entertain and was always ready for
people to drop by. She would call on the spur of the
moment and say, "Come by for some Hanky-Panky."

1 pound mild *or* spicy Jimmy Dean sausage
1 pound ground beef
1 pound Velveeta cheese, cubed
1 package rye *or* pumpernickel cocktail bread

Brown sausage in a skillet; drain and set
aside. Brown beef in the same skillet; drain.
Return sausage to the pan and then add the
cheese. Cook until cheese is melted. Place
spoonfuls onto cocktail bread. You can place
them on a baking sheet in the oven for a few
minutes until well heated and browned on
top. Serve warm.

Instead of heating all at once, you may freeze
some of the snacks for later use. Place on a
baking sheet and put into freezer. When
frozen, place in a ziplock bag and store in
the freezer. Pull out the number desired and
heat on a baking sheet.

the tradition of the king's cake

More like a large round sweet roll or brioche than a cake, the King's Cake is covered with icing or sprinkles in the traditional Mardi Gras colors of green, gold and purple.

Guests need to be warned that a tiny baby (likely the Christ Child in origin) or coin is placed in the dough—the person who finds it in his or her slice must throw the next party...or at least bring the King's Cake (that is, if he or she doesn't choke).

Instead of buying a King's Cake or making a traditional one, you can simply make a yellow cake or pound cake (such as Cream Cheese Pound Cake on page 109) and sprinkle the top with green, gold and purple sprinkles or colored sugar. Don't forget to place a coin or a tiny doll (a facsimile of Baby Jesus) in the batter.

Doris Heard, who grew up in New Orleans, recalls the time she went to a Mardi Gras party as a teen and her mother advised her to swallow the baby so she wouldn't have to hostess the next party!

After Doris' marriage, she brought home a King Cake from New Orleans to Houston, where her husband is a radiologist. He'd take the cake to share at the office, and the staff would X-ray the cake to see where the lucky charm was!

here are our very favorite cajun seafood recipes.

she-crab soup

MARGARET GRIFFITH

3/4 to 1 cup unsalted butter
1 cup finely chopped celery
1/2 cup grated onion
2 cups finely sliced scallions (white part only)
3/4 cup all-purpose flour
7 cups whole milk
7 cups chicken stock
White pepper, ground mace and
   Worcestershire sauce to taste
3 pounds fresh lump crabmeat, picked over
2 cups heavy cream
1/2 cup sherry
Chopped scallions (the green part),
   chopped hard-boiled egg yolks and paprika
Melt butter in a double boiler. Add the celery and onion; sweat for 10 minutes. Add scallions. Slowly add the flour, whisking as

you go. Bubble for 3 minutes. Heat the milk and the stock separately. Add to the vegetable mixture, continuing to stir for another 10 minutes. This is 23 minutes total so far. Add the seasonings to taste. Add the crabmeat. Bring back to a simmer for 1 minute. Add cream and sherry. Bring back to a simmer for 2 minutes. Serve with a garnish of scallions, yolks and paprika.

SERVES 15 AS A FIRST COURSE

crab and corn chowder

ELLEN MORRIS

A low-calorie, high-fiber, fast, easy and fresh recipe. Ginger lovers will want to add an extra teaspoon.

1 bag (16 ounces) frozen petite white corn
   (do not thaw), *divided*
1 cup low-fat milk
1 bottle (8 ounces) clam juice
4 tablespoons sliced green onions, *divided*
1 teaspoon minced peeled fresh
   gingerroot, *divided*
4-1/2 teaspoons lemon juice, *divided*
Salt and pepper to taste
2 tablespoons butter
4 ounces cooked crabmeat, flaked

Reserve 1/4 cup corn. In a saucepan, bring milk and remaining corn to a boil. Cover and remove from the heat; let stand for 10 minutes. Purée mixture in a blender. Add clam juice, 3 tablespoons green onions and 1/2 teaspoon ginger; purée again until almost smooth. Return purée to saucepan; bring to a simmer. Stir in 1-1/2 teaspoons lemon juice. Season with salt and pepper. Melt butter in a small skillet over medium heat. Add reserved corn; sauté for 1 minute. Add crab and remaining onions, ginger and lemon juice; stir until just warm. Ladle soup into bowls; top each with a pretty mound of crab/corn mixture in the center.

SERVES 4 AS A FIRST COURSE

crawfish fettuccine

DORIS HEARD

This is the easy crawfish recipe my sister, Elaine, uses all the time. It came from her good friend who owns a catering business in Lafayette. Crawfish tails are fairly easy to find in the stores. They come in 1-pound packages ready to use in any recipe. However, you can substitute shrimp.

2 large onions, chopped
2 small green bell peppers, chopped
2 cloves garlic, chopped
1 cup butter
1/2 cup all-purpose flour
2 to 3 cups half-and-half cream
1-1/2 cups (6 ounces) shredded
  cheddar cheese
2 pounds cooked crawfish tails
2 tablespoons Creole seasoning
1 pound fettuccine, cooked al dente
1/4 cup thinly sliced green onion tops

In a large saucepan, sauté onions, green peppers and garlic in butter until clear. Add flour; stir until absorbed. Slowly add 2 cups cream, stirring constantly. Add cheese and stir occasionally. Season crawfish tails with Creole seasoning. When cheese is melted and sauce is well blended, add crawfish. Stir slowly; simmer for 5-8 minutes. Add more cream if needed. Toss with cooked fettuccine; cover with onion tops.

SERVES 8

crab cakes

I pound fresh small-size crabmeat
I pound fresh large-size crabmeat
1/2 cup light mayonnaise
1/2 cup chopped fresh flat-leaf parsley
Juice of 2 lemons
I egg
I teaspoon Dijon mustard (or more)
I to 3 teaspoons Old Bay Seasoning
I teaspoon coarse salt
1/4 teaspoon freshly ground pepper
I cup fine bread crumbs
3 to 4 tablespoons unsalted butter, melted
Tartar sauce and lemon wedges

Preheat broiler, with rack 4 inches from heat. Keeping each pound of crabmeat separate, turn out onto paper towels; pick through to remove any shells or cartilage. In a large bowl, stir together the mayonnaise, parsley, lemon juice, egg, mustard, Old Bay, salt and pepper. Add bread crumbs and small-size crabmeat; stir well to combine. Gently fold in large-size crabmeat just until combined. Dividing evenly, form mixture into 8 cakes. Place on a foil-lined baking sheet; drizzle with butter. Broil for 12-15 minutes or until golden brown and warmed throughout (move to lower shelf if tops brown too quickly). Serve with tarter sauce and lemon wedges.

To make ahead: Arrange crab cakes in a waxed paper-lined container so they do not touch; separate layers with waxed paper. Cover and refrigerate up to I day.

SERVES 8

Wine Recommendation: Sauvignon Blanc, Brennan Vineyards Viognier, Australian or New Zealand Riesling

shrimp and grits

BETH WRAY

The late Bill Neal influenced young chefs across the South, and diners still enjoy his inspired recipes at Crook's Corner—a landmark restaurant in Chapel Hill, North Carolina. Executive Chef Bill Smith has added some creative touches to the menu, such as Warm Goat Cheese Salad with Roasted Beets and Pumpkin Seeds, and Hanger Steak with Bourbon Brown Sauce, but Shrimp and Grits is still a Crook's Corner classic.

2 cups water
1 can (14 ounces) chicken broth
3/4 cup half-and-half cream
3/4 teaspoon salt
1 cup quick-cooking grits
3/4 cup shredded cheddar cheese
1/4 cup grated Parmesan cheese
2 tablespoons butter
3/4 teaspoon hot sauce, *divided*
1/4 teaspoon white pepper
3 bacon strips
1 pound medium shrimp,
  peeled and deveined
1/4 teaspoon black pepper
1/8 teaspoon salt
1/4 cup all-purpose flour
1 cup sliced fresh mushrooms
1/2 cup chopped green onions
2 cloves garlic, minced

1/2 cup low-sodium, fat-free chicken broth
2 tablespoons lemon juice
Lemon wedges

In a saucepan, bring the water, broth, cream and salt to a boil; gradually whisk in grits. Reduce heat; simmer for 10 minutes or until thickened, stirring occasionally. Add the cheeses, butter, 1/2 teaspoon hot sauce and white pepper; keep warm.

Cook bacon in a large skillet until crisp; remove to paper towels. Reserve 1 tablespoon drippings in skillet. Crumble bacon and set aside. Sprinkle shrimp with black pepper and salt; dredge in flour. Sauté mushrooms in hot drippings for 5 minutes or until tender. Add green onions and sauté for 2 minutes. Add shrimp and garlic; sauté for 2 minutes or until shrimp are lightly browned. Stir in low-sodium broth, lemon juice and remaining hot sauce; cook 2 more minutes, stirring to loosen bits from bottom of skillet. Serve shrimp mixture over cheese grits. Top with crumbled bacon; serve with lemon wedges.

SERVES 4

shrimp divine (dee'vine)

MARGARET GRIFFITH

The key to this recipe lies in the stock! I don't bother with this recipe anymore unless I have heads-on shrimp, locally available frozen at Fiesta. Preparation: Approximately 2 hours, low intensity!

2 pounds freshest possible shrimp
    (with heads on)
1 onion, quartered
3 to 4 cloves garlic
1 to 2 carrots, cut into medium pieces
2 to 3 whole cloves

sauce:

2 tablespoons tomato paste
Heavy cream
Red, white and black pepper to taste
3/4 cup butter, *divided*
10 cloves garlic, chopped
5 chiles (Arbol, pequín *or* jalapeño),
    chopped
Olive oil
1/2 cup red wine
1 cup chopped flat-leaf parsley (or more)

Put the shrimp heads and shells in a pot; add onion, garlic, carrots and cloves. Fill the pot with water and then simmer; top off. When you smell it starting to burn, add more water and simmer for another 30-45 minutes. Strain first through a colander and then through cheesecloth. The flavor should be strong, the color a dark reddish/brown. Further reduce if necessary down to 1-1/2 to 2 cups.

To the reduced stock, add tomato paste. Stir over heat until smooth. Add cream until you have your desired consistency. Season with red, white and black pepper. In a small saucepan, heat 1/4 cup butter; simmer the garlic and chiles for 5-10 minutes (don't let them get crispy). Add to the sauce.

Lightly cover the shrimp in oil. Heat a cast-iron skillet until very hot; add shrimp. (They will cook quickly in the dry skillet. Use a spatula to keep them from sticking, and don't overcook. The hotter the skillet, the more grilled appearance the shrimp will have.) Remove shrimp. Keeping the heat on high, add remaining butter to the skillet; let it foam up and brown a touch. Add wine and scrape the skillet with your spatula. Add parsley. Cook 30 seconds or so, using a spatula to deglaze the skillet. Add the shrimp and sauce; combine and serve. Good on toast, rice or pasta.

SERVES 2-3

Wine Recommendation: Messina Hof Sauvignon Blanc or a Riesling

chicken gumbo

JAN WALLACE

1/2 cup plus 2 tablespoons canola oil, *divided*
1/2 cup all-purpose flour
2 pounds chicken breasts and thighs
4 quarts water
3 large onions, chopped
1/2 cup chopped green bell pepper
1/2 cup sliced celery
2 to 3 cloves garlic, minced
1 bunch green onions, chopped
1-1/2 pounds sliced fresh *or* frozen okra
1 can (14.5 ounces) diced tomatoes with juice
1 teaspoon brown sugar
1/2 cup chopped fresh parsley
1/2 teaspoon Worcestershire sauce
1/2 teaspoon Tabasco (or to taste)
1/2 teaspoon dried thyme
Salt to taste
Crushed red pepper flakes, optional
2 to 3 drops lemon juice, optional

Heat 1/2 cup oil in a heavy pan. Add flour and stir to make a dark roux (be careful not to burn). Meanwhile, in a large pot, cook chicken in water; reserve stock in the pot. Skim off any fat. Cut chicken into small pieces; set aside. Brown onions, green pepper, celery and garlic in remaining oil, then add green onions and okra. Add this mixture to the reserved stock. Stir in the tomatoes, brown sugar, parsley, Worcestershire sauce, Tabasco and thyme. Simmer for 2-1/2 hours. Add chicken; cook 30 minutes more. Season with salt, pepper flakes and lemon juice if desired. Serve over hot rice.

SERVES 20

Wine Recommendation: Messina Hof Mama Rosa Rosé or a Côtes du Rhône

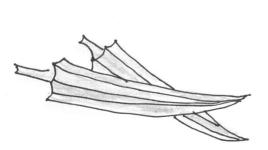

g'damned eggplant

LUCY GOODRICH

2 slices stale bread
1/2 cup heavy cream *or* half-and-half
3 large eggplants, peeled and cubed
5 tablespoons butter, *divided*
1 tablespoon olive oil
3/4 cup chopped yellow onion
1/2 cup chopped green bell pepper
1/2 cup chopped celery
2 large cloves garlic, minced
1 egg, beaten
1 teaspoon salt
1 teaspoon pepper
1/2 teaspoon cayenne pepper
1 tablespoon *each* minced fresh basil and
   thyme *or* 1 teaspoon dried basil and thyme
1 sleeve saltines, crumbled
1/2 cup grated Parmesan cheese
Lemon wedges

Preheat oven to 350°. In a bowl, soak bread in cream. Meanwhile, cook eggplant in boiling salted water until tender, about 10 minutes. Drain well and place in a large bowl. In a sauté pan, heat 1 tablespoon butter and oil. Sauté onion, green pepper and celery until they begin to soften. Add garlic, stirring so it doesn't brown. Add to eggplant. Add beaten egg to bread and cream; combine, using a fork to break up the bread. Pour this over the eggplant mixture and mix well. Add salt, pepper, cayenne, basil and thyme.

Taste it, finesse it and transfer to a shallow ovenproof serving dish. Toss saltine crumbs and Parmesan; sprinkle over the top. Melt remaining butter; drizzle over crackers and cheese. Cover loosely with foil. Bake for 30 minutes. Uncover; bake 10-12 minutes longer. Serve with lemon wedges.

SERVES 4-6

jane's vinaigrette

LUCY GOODRICH

Use this simple vinaigrette with any salad. I like to toss it with crisp romaine and ripe slivers of fresh avocado and serve with crawfish pie.

2/3 cup olive oil
1/3 cup red wine vinegar
2 cloves garlic, crushed
1 teaspoon paprika
1/2 teaspoon dry mustard
Salt and pepper to taste

Combine all ingredients in a jar with a tight-fitting lid; seal and shake well before using.

Eco Tip: Grind the Christmas tree for next year's mulch…or do as the New Orleanians do—redecorate the tree with beads and masks and party on until Lent. If you do the latter, keep your tree well watered and add some 7-Up or vodka to keep the tree happy longer.

RODEO TIME IN HOUSTON

Rodeo time is "Go Western" time. Although the weather is almost always rainy in early February when the trail riders converge on Memorial Park in Houston, it never dampens the spirit or the barbecue fires in front of the chuck wagons. Trail riders ride for miles to come to kick off the great parade downtown. Chili and barbecue cook-offs are the rage as Texans celebrate their Western heritage. "Texas is where the West begins and the East peters out"…or so it's been said.

Spicy sauces from south of the border put a spike into cowboy and cowgirl fare. Ribs, beans, chili, enchiladas, tamales and queso hit the spot at this time of year, served with a cold Shiner Bock (made right here in Shiner, Texas) or cerveza of your choice.

Casual clothing and parties are the rule. Everyone wears jeans, the official attire of cowboys—drugstore and otherwise. And colorful bandanas, found cheaply at dollar stores, serve dual duty as neckwear and napkins.

beth's cowboy chili

KAREN TERRELL

This recipe is from my sister's cookbook, "Our Family's Recipes", which she made in scrapbook fashion—complete with stickers, cutouts, trims, pockets and designer papers—for my brother and me. She has been a cook since she was 9 years old. She surpassed me almost immediately!

2 tablespoons olive oil
1 onion, chopped
1 pound ground beef
1 pound ground sausage
3 cans (14.5 ounces *each*) diced *or* crushed tomatoes
2 cans (15 ounces *each*) red kidney beans, rinsed and drained
1 can (15 ounces) tomato sauce
1 bottle (12 ounces) beer
1 cup water
1 can (4 ounces) diced green chiles
3 tablespoons chili powder
2 tablespoons white vinegar
1 tablespoon Worcestershire sauce
4 bay leaves
3 teaspoons sugar
1 teaspoon dried oregano
1 teaspoon ground cumin
1/2 teaspoon cayenne pepper (or to taste)
Pinch of ground cinnamon

In a large skillet, heat oil. Cook onion until soft and translucent. Add beef and sausage; cook until browned. Transfer to a large pot. Add the rest of the ingredients. Bring to a boil; immediately turn heat down to low. Simmer for several hours until volume has decreased by a quarter. Stir occasionally and add more water if needed. Serve with shredded cheddar cheese, sour cream, chopped jalapeños and cornbread.

SERVES 6

Beverage Recommendation: your favorite beer...for wine, Cabernet Sauvignon or Shiraz

chicken enchiladas with tomatillo salsa

MIMI KERR

3 pounds tomatillos, washed, shucked
  and stems removed
2 jalapeños
1 small onion, quartered
4 cloves garlic, crushed
1/2 bunch cilantro
1 teaspoon salt
20 corn tortillas
1 roasted chicken, skin removed
  and shredded
3 cups (12 ounces) shredded
  Monterey Jack cheese

Combine tomatillos, jalapeños, onion and garlic in a saucepan. Add enough water to cover by 2 inches. Bring to a boil; reduce heat and simmer for 30 minutes or until tomatillos are very soft. Drain. For a milder salsa, remove jalapeños and cut in half; discard seeds and white pith. For a spicier salsa, leave jalapeños whole and do not remove seeds. Place drained tomatillo mixture in the bowl of a food processor. Add cilantro and salt; process until smooth. Taste for seasoning.

Preheat oven to 300°. Wrap tortillas in paper towels and microwave for 1 to 1-1/2 minutes to soften. Place about 3 tablespoons of shredded chicken in the center of each tortilla; add about 1 tablespoon tomatillo salsa. Roll up tightly. Place seam side down in a lightly greased 13-inch x 9-inch x 2-inch baking dish. Pour remaining salsa over enchiladas to cover lightly; sprinkle with cheese. Cover with foil; bake for 15 minutes. Uncover; bake 5 minutes longer or until heated through.

SERVES 10

Wine Recommendation: for white, Dry Comal Creek Vineyards Sauvignon Blanc...for red, an American Shiraz

larry beans

MIKKI PHILLIPS

All cowboys eat beans. These are great for an informal party such as barbecue. Tangy!

1 can (28 ounces) Bush's Baked Beans
1 can (16 ounces) Trappey's
　Jalapeño Navy Beans
1/2 cup ketchup
1 teaspoon yellow mustard
1 teaspoon A-1 sauce
1 teaspoon Heinz 57 sauce
1 teaspoon Hatch Farm *or* Trappey's
　Jalapeño Sauce
1/2 teaspoon pepper
1/4 teaspoon garlic salt

Combine all ingredients in a pot. Simmer for 2 hours or more, stirring occasionally.

MAKES ABOUT 1-1/2 QUARTS

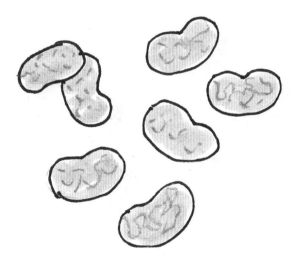

PRESIDENTS' DAY

The third Monday in February is mainly a government holiday and a break for schoolchildren, but we like to honor the father of our country.

cherry cheese cake

DELBY WILLINGHAM

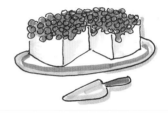

Great for observing George Washington's birthday or for a Valentine's Day party. Kids especially love the mini tarts.

2 cups graham cracker crumbs
6 tablespoons sugar
6 tablespoons butter, melted
1 can (14 ounces) sweetened condensed milk
1/3 cup lemon juice
1/2 pint heavy cream, whipped
1 teaspoon almond extract
1/2 teaspoon vanilla extract
1 can (21 ounces) cherry pie filling

Preheat oven to 375°. Mix graham cracker crumbs with sugar and butter. Pour into a 9-inch square baking pan; press crumb mixture firmly against sides and bottom of pan. Bake for 7 minutes. Cool. With a mixer, beat condensed milk and lemon juice. Fold in whipped cream. Add extracts. Pour over crust; top with cherry pie filling. Refrigerate until serving.

Variation: Make mini tarts by using frozen tart shells; just prick, bake and cool. The recipe makes enough for 16 shells; after filling with the cream mixture, top each with cherry pie filling.

WINTER FAVORITES

Cooler temperatures call for hearty soups and oven meals.

Old Country Favorites ~ Lucy Goodrich

Hungarian Potato Leek Soup and Hungarian Goulash are based upon recipes from the restaurant Gundel in Budapest. Established in the late 1800s, the restaurant was later purchased by Estée Lauder's son, who has poured many millions of dollars into it to keep its place as one of the world's renowned culinary destinations. And what's goulash without noodles? Try my Little Pinched Noodles.

hungarian potato leek soup

1/4 cup unsalted butter
I large potato, peeled and sliced
I artichoke heart, sliced
1/2 rib celery, sliced
1/2 leek, sliced
I tablespoon all-purpose flour
2 cups chicken broth
I cup milk
1/2 cup heavy cream
Salt and freshly ground white pepper to taste
Smoked ham *or* beef tongue and fresh
   mushrooms, cut into thin strips
   for garnish

Melt butter in a 2-quart pot. Sauté the
potato, artichoke heart, celery and leek over
medium heat for 5 minutes. Dust with flour;
stir and add the broth, milk and cream.
Season with salt and white pepper. Simmer
for 40-50 minutes, stirring frequently. In
batches, blend the soup in a blender until
smooth. Transfer to a clean pot; reheat if
necessary. Serve the soup in heated cups;
garnish with ham and mushroom strips.

SERVES 4

hungarian goulash

6 tablespoons vegetable oil, *divided*
I cup finely chopped onion
2 cloves garlic, crushed
2 tablespoons sweet Hungarian paprika
1/2 teaspoon ground caraway seed
3 cups water
1-1/2 pounds veal bones, cut into 2-inch
   pieces (ask butcher!)
Salt to taste
I tomato, peeled, seeded and diced
I yellow bell pepper, diced
I small hot pepper, seeded and
   diced, optional
1-3/4 pounds beef tenderloin, cut into
   I-inch cubes
Little Pinched Noodles (recipe on next page)
   or other cooked noodles

In a frying pan, heat 3 tablespoons oil over
medium-high heat. Add onion and garlic;
sauté for 10 minutes or until golden brown.
Remove from the heat. Stir in the paprika,
caraway seed and water. Add veal bones.
Season with salt. Cook over low heat for
I hour. Replace the water that evaporates
so you end up with 2 cups of sauce. Remove
the bones. Add the tomato, yellow pepper
and hot pepper if desired; simmer for 15
minutes. If the sauce is too thin, increase

the heat to medium and cook for a few minutes until thickened. Transfer the sauce to a smaller pan; cover and keep warm.

In a large frying pan, heat remaining oil over medium-high heat. Add the beef; season lightly with salt. Cook and stir for 4-5 minutes or until browned on the outside but still pink on the inside (do not crowd the pan). Put the meat on warm plates and pour the sauce over it. Top with noodles and serve immediately.

SERVES 4

Wine Recommendation: Messina Hof Shiraz

little pinched noodles

These egg noodles—also called spaetzle—are easy to make and much tastier than store-bought pasta. The first time you make them, they could look ugly but still taste delicious. With practice, they will look nice.

2/3 to 1 cup all-purpose flour
1 egg
Salt
6 cups water *or* chicken broth

Sift 2/3 cup flour into a bowl. Make a well in the center and crack the egg into it. Sprinkle with salt and knead until a stiff dough forms. Add the remaining flour if the dough is not stiff enough. Turn dough onto a lightly floured work surface; pinch flat, rounded, fingernail-size bits from the dough, occasionally sprinkling with flour. Cook in simmering salted water or broth for 10-12 minutes or until noodles rise to the surface.

SERVES 4

pork shoulder roast

KATHY LOVE

Serve with wild rice or couscous to which you've added dried cherries or cranberries.

1 pork shoulder roast (5 to 6 pounds)
2 tablespoons rubbed sage
1 tablespoon ground nutmeg
1/3 cup olive oil
1 clove garlic, minced
1 cup beef broth
3/4 cup red wine
2 tablespoons Dijon mustard
1 tablespoon balsamic vinegar
2 bay leaves
1 tablespoon dried parsley flakes
2 tablespoons cornstarch

Preheat oven to 300°. Rub roast with sage and then sprinkle with nutmeg. Heat oil in a Dutch oven; brown the roast. Add garlic and cook until browned. Add the broth, wine, mustard, vinegar, bay leaves and parsley. Cover and bake for 4 hours. Remove from oven and take roast out of the pot; keep warm. Discard bay leaves. Add cornstarch to cooking liquid using a wire whisk; heat until thickened. Slice roast and serve with gravy.

FEEDS A CROWD

Wine Recommendation: for red, Sunset Vineyards "Moon Glow" Merlot...for white, Chardonnay or Viognier

chestnut soup

PAULINE BOLTON

1/2 cup chopped onion
1/2 cup chopped celery
1/2 cup chopped carrot
2 to 3 tablespoons butter
8 cups chicken broth
Bouquet garni in cheesecloth pouch*
2 cups water-packed chestnuts, drained
  and crumbled
1/2 cup Madeira (preferably Sercial)
1/2 cup heavy cream

In a soup pot, sauté onion, celery and carrot in butter until soft. Add broth and bouquet garni. Simmer for 20-30 minutes. Add chestnuts and Madeira; simmer 3-5 minutes longer. Remove herb pouch. Purée soup in a blender; return to the pan. Stir in cream; heat through (do not boil).

* Use 2 sprigs parsley, 2 sprigs thyme, 1 bay leaf, 3 peppercorns and 1 clove.

SERVES 6-8

roasted cauliflower with pasta

MARY GRACE HAMILL

1 very large head cauliflower (about
  3 pounds), cut into florets
3 cloves garlic, thinly sliced
3 tablespoons olive oil, *divided*
1/4 cup butter, melted
1-3/4 teaspoons salt
1 pound whole-wheat penne pasta
1/2 pound thinly sliced salami
1/4 cup capers
1/4 cup pine nuts, toasted
Grated Parmesan cheese
3 tablespoons chopped fresh flat-leaf parsley
1 log (4 ounces) goat cheese

Preheat oven to 450°. Toss cauliflower and garlic with 2 tablespoons oil, butter and salt; place in a jelly-roll pan. Roast for 25 minutes or until soft and somewhat browned. Meanwhile, cook the pasta according to package directions. Drain and place in a very large skillet; add the roasted cauliflower, salami, capers, pine nuts and remaining oil. Toss well and transfer to a serving dish. Top with Parmesan and parsley. Cut goat cheese into slices to place a slice on each serving; it makes this really special.

SERVES 4-6

Variation: Serve the roasted cauliflower without pasta. Finely crumble a slice of bread with your fingers; brown in 2 tablespoons olive oil. In a serving dish, layer the roasted cauliflower, bread crumbs and 5 tablespoons chopped parsley. Serve warm or at room temperature.

shaved brussels sprouts with pecorino

ELLEN MORRIS

This is a delicious, crunchy slaw–like salad.

6 fresh Brussels sprouts
1 radish
1/3 cup grated Pecorino cheese
3 tablespoons olive oil
2 tablespoons Champagne vinegar *or*
  lemon juice
Salt and pepper to taste

Slice Brussels sprouts and radish very thin.
Chop with a knife on a cutting board to
create a fine slaw; place in a bowl. Add
cheese, oil and vinegar; toss well. Season
with salt and pepper and serve.

maple syrup pie

MARGARET GRIFFITH

1-2/3 cups packed light brown sugar
2 eggs
1/2 cup heavy cream
1/3 cup pure maple syrup (dark amber)
2 teaspoons unsalted butter, melted
1 pie shell
Crème fraîche *or* whipped cream for serving

Preheat oven to 350° with rack in lower third
of oven. In a mixing bowl, whisk the brown
sugar and eggs until creamy. Add cream,
syrup and butter; whisk until smooth. Pour
into pie shell. Bake for 50-60 minutes.
Pastry will be golden and filling puffed with a
little wiggle. Cool. Serve with crème fraîche
or whipped cream.

SERVES 6-8

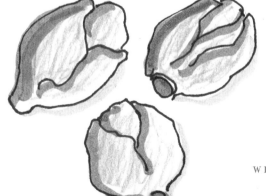

melinda's pie crust

LUCY GOODRICH

This recipe makes a single crust. If you are making a covered fruit pie, double the recipe.

1 cup all-purpose flour
1 teaspoon salt
1/3 cup shortening
1/4 cup ice water

Sift enough flour with no salt, then measure 1 cup of that flour and resift with the salt added. Place in a bowl; cut in shortening. Add ice water; stir quickly and lightly with a fork. Form into a loose ball with your hands. Refrigerate for 30 minutes.

Place the ball of dough on a floured tea towel; using a rolling pin, roll the dough out with as few strokes as possible, making it large enough to hang over the edge of the pie pan a little, so you may make a decorative pattern along the edge (either with the tines of a fork or your thumb and forefinger).

ST. PATRICK'S DAY

The day for the wearin' o' the green is also a day for eating Irish foods! Along with
the hearty sides, soup and salad we share, you can make special sweets simply by
using shamrock-shaped muffin or cake tins and cookie cutters. For some eatin' o'
the green, add a bit of green food coloring to sugar cookie dough...frost with green
frosting or sprinkle with green colored sugar.

colcannon

GAY ESTES

Serve this traditional Irish potato-and-cabbage dish
with corned beef.

2 pounds Yukon Gold potatoes, peeled
   and quartered
1-1/2 cups chopped kale
1/4 cup chopped yellow onion
1/2 to 1 cup unsalted butter,
   room temperature
1/2 to 1 cup whole milk, room temperature
Salt and pepper to taste

Cook potatoes in a large pot of boiling water
for 20-40 minutes or until tender. Drain,
reserving water in the pan. Place potatoes in
a large warmed bowl and keep warm. Add
kale and onion to the potato water. Cook
over medium heat for 6-8 minutes or until
tender; drain. Mash the potatoes with a hand
masher or rice them in a potato ricer. Beat
in the butter, then beat in the milk. Mix in
the kale and onion. Season with salt and
pepper. Beat until fluffy.

SERVES 4

fried cabbage

MARJORIE CRAWFORD

3 bacon strips, chopped
1/4 cup chopped onion
6 cups purple *or* green cabbage, cut into
   thin wedges
2 tablespoons water
Pinch of sugar
Salt and pepper to taste
1 tablespoon cider vinegar*

Place bacon in a large deep skillet. Cook over medium-high heat until browned and crisp (watch carefully so it doesn't burn). Remove bacon but reserve drippings. Cook onion in the hot drippings until tender. Add cabbage; stir in water, sugar, salt and pepper. Cook until cabbage wilts, about 15 minutes. Stir in bacon. Splash with vinegar; toss and serve.

I sometimes add more vinegar just because we like the tangy taste.

SERVES 6

jule's mashed turnips

MARY TRAINER

1 large turnip, peeled and cubed
3 sweet potatoes, peeled and cubed
1/4 cup milk
2 tablespoons unsalted butter
1/2 teaspoon sugar
3/4 teaspoon salt
1/4 teaspoon pepper
2 tablespoons crumbled goat cheese

Place turnips and sweet potatoes in a large pot; cover with water. Bring to a boil; cook for 25 minutes or until tender. Drain. Preheat oven to 375°. Mash the turnips and potatoes with milk, butter, sugar, salt and pepper until slightly lumpy. Transfer to a small baking dish. Cover with goat cheese (use extra if desired—it never hurt anybody). Cover loosely and bake for 15 minutes. Uncover and continue baking for 8 minutes or until lightly browned.

SERVES 6

garlic mashed potatoes

MARY TRAINER

3-3/4 pounds red potatoes, peeled
    and cubed
9 large cloves garlic
2 tablespoons butter
2 tablespoons minced fresh rosemary *or*
    2 teaspoons dried rosemary, crushed
1 cup low-sodium chicken broth
1/2 cup grated Parmesan cheese

Place potatoes and garlic in a saucepan and cover with water; boil for 20 minutes or until tender. Drain. Mash with butter and rosemary, using an electric mixer. Heat broth; gradually add to potatoes. Stir in Parmesan.

SERVES 6

split pea with ham soup

MARY TRAINER

2 cups dried split peas
2 quarts chicken broth
2 cups water
1 ham hock
1/4 cup olive oil
1 cup finely chopped onion
1/2 cup grated carrots
1/2 cup diced celery
1 clove garlic, minced
1/4 cup minced fresh parsley
2-1/2 teaspoons salt
1/2 teaspoon freshly ground pepper
Pinch of dried basil
1 bay leaf
1 cup milk
1 cup diced cooked ham

Wash the peas and soak for 1 hour in warm water; drain. In an 8-quart pot, bring broth and water to a boil. Add the peas and ham hock. Simmer for 2-1/2 hours, stirring occasionally. Remove ham hock; when cool enough to handle, cut any meat off the bones and set aside.

In a large skillet, heat oil; sauté the onion, carrots, celery and garlic for 10 minutes. Add to the peas along with the parsley, salt, pepper, basil and bay leaf. Simmer for 30-50 minutes more, stirring occasionally. Remove and discard bay leaf. Purée the soup in batches in a blender. Return the soup to the pot; stir in milk, diced ham and reserved ham. Gently reheat 10-15 minutes before serving.

SERVES 8

baked creamed spinach

ESTHER GLOVER

1 tablespoon olive oil
3/4 cup minced onion
2 teaspoons minced garlic
2 packages (10 ounces *each*) frozen chopped
   spinach, thawed and drained
2 packages (12 ounces *each*) Stouffer's frozen
   spinach soufflés, thawed
1/4 teaspoon ground nutmeg
Freshly ground pepper

Preheat oven to 350°. Heat oil in a large
nonstick skillet. Add onion and garlic; cook
until onion softens. Meanwhile, squeeze
thawed spinach to release some of the liquid
but not all. Add spinach to onion and garlic;
mix well. Cook until heated through.
Remove from the heat. Stir in spinach
soufflés, nutmeg and pepper. Transfer to a
greased shallow 5-cup baking dish. Spread
smooth with a spatula. Can be made up to
this point up to 2 days ahead and refrigerated. Bake, uncovered, for 45 minutes or
until edges are bubbling and surface is a
darker green but not brown.

SERVES 8

spinach salad

MARY TRAINER

1 pound romaine
1/2 pound baby spinach
1/2 pound fresh mushrooms, sliced
3 green onions, sliced
6 bacon strips, cooked and crumbled
6 tablespoons salad oil
2 tablespoons lemon juice
1 egg yolk*
1 clove garlic, pressed
3/4 teaspoon salt
1/4 teaspoon pepper
1/8 teaspoon dry mustard

In a large salad bowl, toss the romaine,
spinach, mushrooms, green onions and
bacon. In a small bowl, whisk the oil,
lemon juice, egg yolk, garlic, salt, pepper
and mustard. Pour over salad and toss;
serve immediately.

*If you prefer to not use uncooked egg in the dressing,
just leave it out; the dressing will be thinner.*

SERVES 4

OSCAR NIGHT

*Hosting a gathering to watch the Academy Awards? These dishes
are winners in our book.*

Oscar Night Party ~ Lucy Goodrich

*My oldest daughter, Caroline Frost, developed
these recipes.*

*This menu features: Bourbon Ginger Ale, Sautéed
Pork Meatballs with Cran-Apple Relish, Double
Butternut Squash and Mexican Hot Chocolate. A nice
addition to the meal is Caroline's Tandoori Chicken
Drumsticks (recipe on page 240).*

bourbon ginger ale

10 cups ginger ale *or* ginger beer
16 jiggers bourbon
4 tablespoons lemon juice
2 tablespoons freshly grated ginger juice*

Mix all ingredients in a pitcher and serve
over ice.

** Ginger juice is the liquid rendered from freshly grated
ginger. I grate a knob and squeeze the juice from my
fist, but you could also use cheesecloth. It adds a sharp,
refreshing kick to the sweet, smooth bourbon cocktail.*

sautéed pork meatballs with cran-apple relish

This meatball recipe can be done several different ways, depending on your mood. I make a bunch and freeze what I don't use on a cookie sheet, then store in a double freezer bag for another day. They can be dropped into boiling broth with white beans and Swiss chard...wrapped in wonton wrappers for dumplings...folded into grape leaves and steamed...or floured, browned and simmered in tomato sauce for spaghetti and meatballs.

You can serve also the meatballs with chutney, but the relish is perfectly simple and worth the extra 10 minutes it takes to make at home.

1 small yellow onion, finely chopped
2 to 4 tablespoons olive oil, *divided*
1 pound ground pork
1 cup steamed brown rice
1 egg
1/2 cup chopped green onions
1/2 cup bread crumbs (or enough to hold
  meat mixture together)
Pinch of Chinese five-spice powder
Salt and pepper to taste

relish:

1/2 cup sugar
1/2 cup water
1 pound cranberries
2 large Gala apples, peeled and diced
1/4 cup chopped walnuts

Sauté onion in a little oil until just translucent; transfer to a large bowl. Add the pork, rice, egg, onions, bread crumbs, five-spice powder, salt and pepper; mix thoroughly. Form into walnut-size balls, small enough to eat in one bite. Heat a cast-iron skillet; brown the meatballs in remaining oil, turning after about 3 minutes a side. Drain on paper towel. Serve hot. These can be made the afternoon of the party and reheated in a 350° oven for 5-10 minutes.

To make the relish: In a large saucepan, bring sugar and water to a boil; cook until sugar is dissolved. Add cranberries and apples; return to a boil, then lower heat to a brisk simmer. Cook for 10-15 minutes or until viscous and syrupy. Cool; garnish with chopped walnuts. Serve meatballs on a platter with the bowl of relish and toothpicks.

double butternut squash

Instead of serving this as a side dish, you could serve it as a meatless main for two along with a simple green salad.

2 large butternut squash, peeled and cubed
1/4 cup butter
Dash of nutmeg
Salt to taste
Shredded Gruyère, optional

Boil the squash in salted water just until tender; drain until dry. In a sauté pan, heat butter until foaming; add squash and cook for 2-3 minutes. Add nutmeg and salt. Serve as is; or transfer to a casserole, top with Gruyère and place in a 450° oven for 5 minutes to brown the top.

SERVES 6

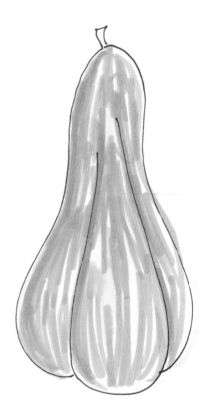

mexican hot chocolate

1 cup cocoa powder

3 cups milk, *divided*

2 cups heavy cream

3/4 cup sugar

2 teaspoons Mexican vanilla extract

1-1/2 teaspoons ground cinnamon

2 pinches of cayenne pepper

4 squares (1 ounce *each*)
   unsweetened chocolate

8 cinnamon sticks for serving

In a large pot, whisk cocoa powder with
1/2-2/3 cup milk until all lumps are gone
and mixture is smooth. Add the cream
and the rest of the milk. Add sugar, vanilla,
cinnamon and cayenne; whisk over medium
heat until steaming, then reduce heat to low.
Melt the chocolate in a microwave-safe bowl;
whisk in few tablespoons of the milky mixture
to temper, adding more as it is incorporated.
Mix the remaining milk mixture into the
bowl. Serve immediately in espresso cups
with cinnamon sticks.

SERVES 8

march garden notes:

* Continue to plant citrus.
* Begin to plant flowers such as
  ageratum, coneflowers, daylilies,
  dianthus and geraniums according
  to HoustonGrows.com.

spectacular spring

spectacular *Spring*

April, May and June bring great weather and the enjoyment of spring bulbs and fresh new growth. You can begin to plant warm-weather plants: begonias, cosmos, marigolds, salvias, succulents and zinnias. It's time to mulch, too. Spring is also the perfect time to bring outdoors indoors, which means flower arranging!

The season is filled with reasons to celebrate: April Fools' Day, Easter, Derby Day, Cinco de Mayo and Mother's Day. For a spring party, fresh flower arrangements for your home are a must. And there's no need to go to the florist. Search your yard, or see what neighbors might have growing that they are willing to share. Here are some things to keep in mind for easy, long-lasting arrangements:

* Collect flowers early in the morning or late in the afternoon when moisture in the flowers is at a maximum. (For sunflowers and other sturdy dry-weather plants, cut them at noon.) If you can cut right after a rain or can water the area first, it helps with the flowers' lasting power.

* Cut more than you think you'll need. Select fresh specimens just about fully opened and avoid new growth, which can't stand the stress of being cut.

* Get everything into water as soon as possible. Flowers need time to recover from cutting (called hardening off), so let them soak overnight or at least for several hours. The flowers will drink the most when freshly cut, so it's important to go back and water an

Spring is the time to bring outdoors indoors.

arrangement about an hour after finishing it. Change the water if you aren't going to make the arrangement that day.

* If you use Oasis floral foam, soak the foam for at least two hours so the center of the block is wet. Just putting the block under the faucet will result in a dry center and disappointing flowers.

* Make a fresh slanted cut with a sharp knife or clippers. Keep everything clean! Take off any foliage you don't need and never let it sit under the water either when conditioning or in the arrangement. Snip off lily stamens to prevent stains. If something wilts, clip it out, don't pull it out!

* Use garden or store vegetables and fruits in your arrangements; they add a great deal to

the spontaneity of the arrangement and can be recycled and eaten later. Use satay sticks or wooden skewers instead of floral picks so they don't spoil the "food."

* A lazy Susan is very helpful. It moves, you stand still, and you finish your creation all the way around, which is good for the balance and full dimension of the arrangement.

* A splash of clear soda pop helps feed the flowers and acts as a mild disinfectant. Commercial plant food is not necessary and can actually overfeed the flowers, causing them to open up and mature too quickly.

* Keep arrangements out of drafts, especially from ceiling fans and vents, as wind dries them out.

APRIL FOOLS' DAY

April Fools' Day is a quasi-holiday with ancient origins: An April Fool was someone who planted his crops before May Day. It is celebrated in many countries with good humor and pranks, oftentimes involving food.

FUN WITH FAUX FOOD

Egg 'Em On: Spread a teaspoon of melted butter on a piece of foil. Melt another teaspoon of butter with 12 mini marshmallows; spread the mixture on the buttered foil and spread out like a fried egg. For the "yolk," press a dried apricot in the center.

Clever Cupcakes: Bake meat loaf in muffin cups at 375° for 15 minutes. For "frosting," use mashed potatoes colored pink with beet juice or red food coloring.

Edible Dominoes: Cut brownies into rectangle shapes and use white icing to draw lines and dots on top to resemble dominoes.

Cheesy Carrots: Roll slices of soft cheese into cone shapes; roll in paprika and insert a sprig of parsley for the carrot top.

Animal Tricks: Make cutout cookies for humans but use a dog bone-shaped cookie cutter so they look like treats for Fido.

hamburger cookies

MIKKI PHILLIPS

With tinted coconut for lettuce...frosting for mayonnaise, ketchup and mustard...vanilla wafers for buns...and chocolate cookies for burgers, these are the sweetest and cutest "sliders" you'll ever try!

1 cup flaked coconut
4 drops green food coloring
3 tubes (4.5 ounces *each*) decorator frosting
    in white, yellow and red
1 package (12 ounces) vanilla wafers
1 package (10 ounces) mint-flavored
    chocolate cookies
1 tablespoon water
2 teaspoons light corn syrup
Sesame seeds

Combine coconut and food coloring in a ziplock bag; seal and shake until evenly colored. Set aside. Squeeze about 1/2 teaspoon white frosting onto the flat side of a vanilla wafer. Top with a chocolate cookie, pressing gently to show frosting around edges. Squeeze about 1/2 teaspoon yellow frosting and 1/2 teaspoon red frosting over chocolate cookie. Sprinkle with 1 teaspoon coconut. Squeeze about 1/2 teaspoon of any color frosting onto the flat side of a second vanilla wafer; place frosting side down over coconut, pressing gently to show frosting around edges. Repeat with remaining cookies, frosting and coconut. When all are assembled, combine water and corn syrup; brush lightly over cookie tops. Sprinkle with sesame seeds and let dry.

MAKES 3 DOZEN

EASTER

Along with Christmas, Easter is our most important religious holiday. It is the end of Lenten fasting and a season of celebration. Families gather after church for a big meal, often featuring spring lamb, carrots (bunny food), deviled eggs and chocolates. Easter also means decorating colorful hard-boiled eggs and hiding them for the children to find. Another fun Easter activity is to make your own sugar egg with a Wilton kit and assemble the scene with miniatures from the craft shop.

painted cookies

MIMI KERR

Make egg and bunny shapes...fun for the kids!

1 cup butter, softened

2 cups sugar

2 eggs

2 teaspoons vanilla extract

4 cups all-purpose flour

2 teaspoons baking powder

1 teaspoon salt

cookie paint:

6 egg yolks

2 teaspoons water

Food coloring in colors of your choice

Several new thin paintbrushes

Candy sprinkles and beads, optional

Using a hand mixer, cream butter and sugar. Add eggs and vanilla; mix well. Sift flour, baking powder and salt; add to creamed mixture and mix well. Work dough with your hands, forming it into a ball. Wrap dough in plastic wrap and refrigerate for 1 hour.

To make the cookie paint: Beat egg yolks and water. Pour into several small bowls; dye with food coloring. Preheat oven to 350°. Sprinkle work surface with sugar and flour to prevent dough from sticking. Roll dough a little over 1/4 inch thick. Cut shapes with a knife or cookie cutters. Place on baking sheets. Generously paint cookies with egg yolk paint (a thin paintbrush works well). Bake for 6-7 minutes or until lightly browned. Decorate with candy sprinkles and beads as desired. Loosen from pan and cool.

MAKES 3 DOZEN

bunny cream biscuits

MIMI KERR

2 cups all-purpose flour
1 tablespoon baking powder
1 tablespoon sugar
1 scant teaspoon salt
1 cup heavy cream
Raisins
Slivered almonds
1 egg white, beaten

Preheat oven to 400°. Lightly coat a baking sheet with nonstick cooking spray or line with parchment paper. In a mixing bowl, combine flour, baking powder, sugar and salt. Add cream and stir until ingredients are lightly blended and hold together. Knead dough a few times with your hands until smooth. On a lightly floured surface, quickly pat dough to 3/4-inch thickness. Cut 1-inch biscuits with a biscuit cutter.

To make bunnies, half of the biscuit rounds will be the heads and the other half will be cut into ears. Place 7 rounds on the prepared baking sheet. Fill a bowl with 1/2 cup water. Cut the remaining 7 rounds in half; shape into ears and flatten one end. Dip the flattened end into water and place under the biscuit rounds. Add raisins for eyes and nose and slivered almonds for whiskers. Brush with egg white. Bake for 12 minutes or until lightly browned, turning baking sheet halfway through baking time. Serve hot.

MAKES 7 BISCUITS

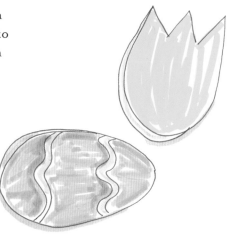

carrot soup with cilantro

MIMI KERR

5 tablespoons unsalted butter
1 large yellow onion, chopped *or* 2 bunches
    leeks (white portion only), chopped
2 pounds baby carrots, chopped
3 cans (14 ounces *each*) chicken broth
1 teaspoon salt
Freshly ground pepper to taste
1 cup (8 ounces) sour cream
1 cup light cream *or* half-and-half
1 tablespoon lemon juice
1/4 cup finely chopped fresh cilantro

In a heavy 4- or 5-quart pot, melt butter over medium heat. Add the onion and sauté for 4 minutes. Add the carrots; sauté 5 minutes more. Add broth, salt and pepper. Simmer, uncovered, for 20 minutes or until vegetables are tender. Remove from the heat. Purée soup in two batches in a food processor; transfer to a bowl. Whisk in the sour cream, light cream, lemon juice and cilantro. Refrigerate until chilled.

warmed chèvre spread with sun-dried tomatoes and basil

MIMI KERR

1 teaspoon olive oil
4 ounces chèvre (goat cheese)
1 package (3 ounces) cream cheese
1/3 cup chopped oil-packed sun-dried
    tomatoes, drained
1/4 cup chopped fresh basil
1/2 teaspoon chopped garlic

Preheat oven to 400°. Lightly coat a small ovenproof serving dish with oil. Crumble chèvre into dish and add chunks of cream cheese. Bake for 10-12 minutes or until soft and melting. Meanwhile, combine the tomatoes, basil and garlic. Remove dish from the oven and stir cheeses together. Top with tomato mixture. Serve hot with crackers or Melba toast.

The Bulb and Plant Mart has many varieties of basil, including sweet, globe and purple; experiment with them in your cooking. Pinch off the flowers for a milder flavor.

easter leg of lamb

SALLY MEADOWS

*This leg of lamb takes a long time to cook, but prep time
is about 30 minutes plus checking once it's placed in the
oven. Don't leave the house!*

1 bunch of thyme
6 medium onions, quartered
6 carrots, quartered
1 whole garlic bulb, peeled and
    separated into cloves
6 bay leaves
1 bone-in leg of lamb (6 to 7 pounds)
Salt and pepper
2 bottles (750 ml *each*) white *or* red wine
3 pounds small red potatoes
3 cans (14.5 ounces *each*) diced tomatoes,
    drained *or* 5 fresh tomatoes, diced

Preheat oven to 350°. Divide the thyme
into four or five parts and tie with kitchen
string. Layer onions, carrots, garlic, bay
leaves and thyme on the bottom of a large
roaster. Place lamb on top. Bake, uncovered,
for 30 minutes. Remove from the oven;
turn lamb over. Season with salt and pepper.
Bake, uncovered, for 30 more minutes.

Place roasting pan on top of the stove,
leaving the oven on. Slowly pour the wine
over the lamb. Bring to a low boil on top of
the stove. Cover roaster with lid and return
to the oven. Bake for 3-5 hours or until
meat is falling off the bone. Check liquid
every hour or so; it should be simmering,
not boiling, or it will evaporate. One hour
before serving, add potatoes and tomatoes to
pan, burying in the cooking juices. It's ready
when the potatoes are cooked. Add more salt
and pepper if needed.

SERVES ABOUT 10

rack of lamb with garlic herb crust and roasted tomatoes

KAREN TERRELL

3 cloves garlic, minced
2 tablespoons minced fresh rosemary *or*
  2 teaspoons dried rosemary, crushed
1-1/2 tablespoons minced fresh thyme *or*
  1-1/2 teaspoons dried thyme
Salt and pepper to taste
1/4 cup olive oil
1/4 cup panko bread crumbs
4 ripe tomatoes, cut in half
1 rack of lamb (8 ribs)

Preheat oven to 450°. In a bowl, smash the garlic, rosemary, thyme, salt and pepper with a pestle. Stir in oil and bread crumbs; mix until it comes together. Sprinkle a small amount of bread crumb mixture on each tomato half; set aside. Place rack of lamb in a roasting pan; press remaining crumb mixture onto fatty side of meat. Tuck tomatoes under lamb so bones are resting on them. Roast for 20 minutes. Reduce oven to 350°. Roast until internal temperature is 137°; roast 3-4 more minutes for medium-rare (145°). Let stand for 5-10 minutes before carving.

SERVES 4

English Sauce from Your Garden: Finely chop 1/2 cup clean mint leaves; add to 1 cup malt vinegar and 2 tablespoons sugar in a saucepan. Simmer for about 20 minutes. Store in a clean container. This lasts for months and makes a wonderful gift in an attractive container. Perfect with lamb and other meats.

oven-roasted sweet potatoes

MARJORIE CRAWFORD

Great combo of sweet and salty! Make as many or as few as you need for the number of people you have coming to dinner.

Sweet potatoes
Olive oil
Ground cumin
Kosher salt

Preheat oven to 400°. Peel sweet potatoes; cut into nuggets or fries. Place in a bowl and toss with enough oil to coat. Sprinkle with cumin and salt. Spread in a single layer on a baking sheet. Bake for 30 minutes or until tender, turning potatoes halfway through baking time.

wine jelly

PAULINE BOLTON

2 envelopes (1/4 ounce *each*)
    unflavored gelatin
1 cup water
1-1/2 cups rosé wine
1/2 cup cranberry juice
1/2 cup sugar
2 tablespoons lemon juice
Mint sprigs for garnish

Soften gelatin in water. In a saucepan, combine the wine, cranberry juice, sugar and lemon juice; cook and stir until sugar is dissolved. Stir in softened gelatin. Cool. Pour into a very lightly oiled 1-quart mold. Refrigerate until firm. Garnish with mint.

carrots with horseradish

DORIS HEARD

Everyone loves these carrots. I sometimes vary the ingredient proportions, and it always comes out great.

1 small bag of carrots, sliced into
    1/4-inch-thick coins
1/2 cup mayonnaise
1 to 2 teaspoons prepared horseradish
3/4 cup crushed Ritz crackers
3 tablespoons butter, melted

Preheat oven to 350°. Steam carrots until just tender; stop the cooking process by covering with ice water. Mix mayonnaise and horseradish. Drain the carrots and toss with the horseradish sauce. Place in a shallow baking dish. Toss the cracker crumbs and butter; sprinkle over carrots. Bake for 20 minutes or until hot.

SERVES 4

heavenly spinach

MARY TRAINER

1/2 pound fresh mushrooms, sliced
6 tablespoons butter, *divided*
1/2 cup mayonnaise
1/2 cup sour cream
1/2 cup grated Parmesan cheese
4 packages (10 ounces *each*) frozen chopped
   spinach, thawed and well drained
1 package (10 ounces) frozen artichoke
   hearts, thawed
Salt and pepper to taste
3 large tomatoes, sliced 1/2 inch thick
1/2 cup dry bread crumbs

Preheat oven to 325°. Sauté mushrooms in
2 tablespoons butter. In a bowl, combine the
mayonnaise, sour cream and Parmesan. Stir
in the mushrooms, spinach and artichokes.
Season with salt and pepper. Pour into a
buttered 13-inch x 9-inch x 2-inch baking
dish. Arrange tomatoes on top. Toast bread
crumbs in remaining butter; sprinkle over
vegetables. Bake for 20 minutes.

SERVES 10

banana cake with penuche icing

MARGARET GRIFFITH

*Decorate the cake plate with edible Easter basket grass
(coconut mixed with a drop of green food coloring)
and candies.*

1 cup unsalted butter, softened
1 cup sugar
2 eggs
1 cup mashed ripe bananas
1-3/4 cups all-purpose flour
2/3 teaspoon baking soda
1/2 teaspoon salt
5 tablespoons buttermilk
2 teaspoons vanilla extract

icing:

1/4 cup butter
1/2 cup packed brown sugar
1/8 teaspoon salt
1/3 cup light cream *or* evaporated milk
2 cups powdered sugar, sifted
1 tablespoon vanilla extract

Preheat oven to 350°. Grease and flour
two 9-inch round cake pans. With a mixer,
cream butter and sugar until light and fluffy.
Add eggs, one at a time, beating well after
each addition. Add bananas; mix well.
Sift flour, baking soda and salt; add to
creamed mixture and stir until completely
incorporated. Add buttermilk and vanilla;
mix for 1 minute. Pour batter into prepared
pans. Bake on the middle oven rack for
23-30 minutes or until sides start pulling
away from the pan and a cake tester comes
out clean. Cool for 10 minutes; remove
cakes from pans and cool on a wire rack
for 2 hours.

For icing, combine butter, brown sugar,
salt and cream in a double boiler; heat and
stir until smooth. Cool slightly. Beat in powdered sugar and vanilla until icing is a good
spreading consistency. Spread between layers
and over top and sides of cake.

SERVES 10-12

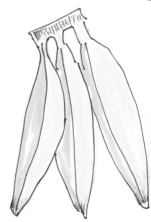

german chocolate cake

DELBY WILLINGHAM

1 package (4 ounces) German sweet chocolate
1/2 cup boiling water
1 cup shortening
2 cups sugar
4 eggs, *separated*
2-1/2 cups cake flour
1 cup buttermilk, *divided*
1 teaspoon baking soda
1 teaspoon vanilla extract
Dash of salt

frosting:

1 cup sugar
1 cup evaporated milk
1/2 cup butter, cubed
3 egg yolks, beaten
1 cup flaked coconut
1/2 to 1 cup chopped pecans
1 teaspoon vanilla extract

Preheat oven to 350°. Grease and flour three 9-inch round cake pans. Melt German chocolate in boiling water. With a mixer, cream shortening and sugar. Add egg yolks, one at a time. Beat in melted chocolate. Alternately add flour and 3/4 cup buttermilk.

Dissolve baking soda in remaining buttermilk; add to batter with vanilla and salt. Fold in stiffly beaten egg whites. Bake for 30 minutes or until a tester comes out clean and edges just start to pull away from pan. Cool for 10 minutes; remove cakes from pans and cool on a wire rack.

For frosting, combine the sugar, evaporated milk, butter and egg yolks in a heavy pan. Cook and stir over low heat until thick. Remove from the heat; stir in coconut, pecans and vanilla until well blended. Spread between cake layers and over top and sides of cake.

SERVES 12-14

Easter lilies are on sale after Easter. Buy one (or more) and put in the garden for next year. The lilies will naturalize. Do not cut off the spent blooms. Collect the seeds and sow for even more plants!

DERBY DAY

The running of the Kentucky Derby happens annually on the first Saturday in May. The "run for the roses" can be a fun party. Watching the 2-minute run—with the 2-hour buildup from stable views to finish line—calls for Kentucky bourbon, mint juleps, fancy hats and our own Cordon Bluegrass Dip.

mint juleps
for a party

CARTER LEE

recipe for 1 julep:

1-1/2 ounces bourbon

2 teaspoons mint juice

1 teaspoon simple syrup

1 ounce water

Combine ingredients and pour over crushed ice in a silver julep cup or glass. Garnish with a sprig of fresh mint.

recipe for 34 juleps:

51 ounces bourbon (2 fifths)*

14 ounces mint juice

7 ounces simple syrup

32 ounces water

Combine ingredients and refrigerate overnight. The mixture is good for several weeks.

mint juice:

Fill blender about three-fourths full with mint leaves; add 1 cup of water. Blend and strain. This makes about 8 ounces of mint juice. Repeat process as many times as needed for the number of drinks you want to make.

simple syrup:

In a saucepan, bring 1 part water plus 1 part sugar to a boil; cool. The amount of simple syrup you make depends on how many drinks you want to make. For example, 5 ounces water plus 5 ounces sugar yields about 7 ounces simple syrup.

* Early Times bourbon is traditional at Churchill Downs. Woodford Reserve is also a favorite.

Do shop the Bulb and Plant Mart for all sorts of herbs. A mint called Kentucky Colonel available there is ideal for this drink.

minted ginger ale cooler

GAIL ANDERSON

1 quart water
1/2 cup sugar
2 cups crushed fresh mint
Juice of 4 lemons
Grated peel of 1 lemon
8 cups ginger ale

In a saucepan, boil water and sugar for 10 minutes. Remove from the heat; stir in mint. Cool. Transfer to a pitcher; add lemon juice and peel. Chill. For each serving, pour 1/4 cup mint syrup over ice; fill the rest of the glass with ginger ale.

SERVES 8

cordon bluegrass dip

RACHEL ALEXANDER

1/4 cup water
2 cloves garlic, chopped
1 pound ricotta cheese
1 pound blue cheese *or* Gorgonzola, crumbled
Dash of hot pepper sauce
Salt to taste
5 fresh sage leaves
1-1/2 cups chopped walnuts, toasted

In a saucepan, heat water and garlic until liquid is reduced to 2 tablespoons. Transfer to a food processor; add cheeses, hot pepper sauce and salt. Process until blended. Place the sage leaves on a double thickness of cheesecloth; place walnuts and cheese mixture on top. Gather the cloth to form a ball and tie together; place in a sieve overnight (with a bowl to catch the draining liquid). Unwrap and invert onto a plate. Serve with crackers or toasts.

SERVES 16

trifecta trout spread

RIVA RIDGE

This spread may be made 2 days in advance.

3 medium russet potatoes
2 cups flaked boneless smoked trout
I clove garlic, crushed
I/4 cup heavy cream
I/4 cup olive oil
Toasts
Chopped fresh parsley *or* paprika for garnish

Preheat oven to 400°. Bake potatoes for
I hour or until tender. When cool enough
to handle, scoop potato pulp out of shells
and place in a food processor. Add the trout,
garlic, cream and oil; process until blended.
Chill for at least 4 hours. To serve, spread
on toasts. Sprinkle a bit of parsley or
paprika on top.

"seabiscuits" will get your party out of the gate

Place a dab of crème fraîche on a potato
chip topped with a dollop of caviar. If you
have more time, make "spoons" out of dry
crusty bread, then top with crème fraîche
and caviar.

spicy bourbon pork tenderloin

LIZ ROTAN

2 pork tenderloins
I egg, lightly beaten
I/2 cup finely chopped pecans
I to 2 teaspoons Cajun *or* Creole seasoning
2 to 3 teaspoons butter

sauce:

I shallot, minced
I clove garlic, minced
I tablespoon butter
I jar (IO ounces) apricot preserves or jam
I/2 cup bourbon

Preheat oven to 450°. Dip tenderloins in
beaten egg, then roll in chopped pecans and
Cajun seasoning. Dot with butter. Place in a
metal baking pan coated with nonstick cooking spray. Bake for I5 minutes. Reduce heat
to 350°. Bake IO minutes longer. Let stand
for IO minutes. Meanwhile, sauté shallot and
garlic in butter (do not brown). Dump in the
jar of apricot preserves. Bring to a boil. Add
bourbon; return to a boil. Pour over pork.

SERVES 4-6

jack daniel's steak sauce

LAURIE LIEDTKE

Olive oil
1 pound fresh mushrooms, sliced
2 shallots, minced
1/4 cup Jack Daniel's whiskey
3/4 cup beef consommé
3 cloves garlic, minced
1 tablespoon Dijon mustard
1 heaping tablespoon mixed peppercorns,
   crushed, optional
1 teaspoon chopped fresh tarragon *or* parsley
Salt to taste
1 cup heavy cream
Flat-leaf parsley for garnish

Heat oil in large skillet (not nonstick); sauté mushrooms and shallots until mushrooms begin to brown, about 5-7 minutes. Add whiskey and consommé; bring to a boil and deglaze pan by scraping up the browned bits. Add garlic, mustard, peppercorns if desired, tarragon and salt; cook for 1 minute. Stir in cream. Bring to a boil; cook until sauce is reduced by half, about 8-10 minutes. Serve hot over steaks. This sauce can be made a day ahead. If it gets too thick, add more cream. Garnish with flat-leaf parsley.

MAKES ABOUT 3 CUPS

corn, cherry tomato, arugula and blue cheese salad

MARGARET GRIFFITH

2 to 3 bunches arugula
2-3/4 cups fresh corn kernels
4 ribs celery, chopped
1 pint cherry tomatoes, halved
1/2 red onion, chopped
2 tablespoons balsamic vinegar
1/3 cup olive oil
Salt and pepper to taste
1 cup (4 ounces) crumbled blue cheese, *divided*

Trim arugula stems and chop the leaves; place in a large bowl. Add the corn, celery, tomatoes and onion. Place vinegar in a small bowl; gradually whisk in oil. Season with salt and pepper. Add 3/4 cup blue cheese. Pour dressing over salad and toss to coat. Top with remaining blue cheese. Cover and refrigerate until serving. Can be prepared 4 hours ahead.

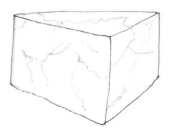

buttermilk pie

MARGARET PIERCE

1-1/2 cups sugar
3 tablespoons all-purpose flour
2 eggs, well beaten
1/2 cup butter, melted
1 cup buttermilk
1 teaspoon vanilla extract
1 teaspoon lemon extract
1 unbaked 9-inch pie shell, chilled

Preheat oven to 425°. In a mixing bowl, combine sugar and flour; stir in eggs. Add butter and buttermilk; mix well. Stir in extracts. Pour into chilled pastry shell. Bake for 10 minutes. Reduce heat to 350°. Bake 35 minutes more. Do not open door while baking. Cover edge of crust with foil or metal shield if crust begins to brown too much.

SERVES 6-8

margaret griffith's buttermilk pie:

Blend 1-3/4 sticks softened butter with 3-3/4 cups sugar and 1/2 cup flour. Add 6 eggs (room temperature), 1-1/2 teaspoons vanilla and 1 cup buttermilk. Pour into 2 unbaked pie shells. Bake at 350° for 40 minutes.

triple crown cookies

AMY ALYDAR

Prepare in the time it takes to saddle a Derby winner!

1 cup butter, softened
1 cup packed brown sugar
1/2 cup sugar
2 eggs
5 tablespoons Kentucky bourbon
2-1/2 cups all-purpose flour
1 teaspoon baking soda
1/2 teaspoon salt
1-1/2 cups chopped pecans
1-2/3 cups semisweet chocolate chips

Preheat oven to 350°. With a mixer, cream butter and sugars. Beat in the eggs slowly; when combined, add the bourbon. Combine the flour, baking soda and salt; add to creamed mixture and mix well. Stir in the pecans and chocolate chips. Drop onto ungreased baking sheets. Bake for 10 minutes. Cool for 1-2 minutes before removing to wire racks.

MAKES 5 DOZEN

CINCO DE MAYO

The fifth of May is not Mexican Independence Day (which is actually
September 16). Rather, it is a celebration of Mexican heritage…recalling
May 5, 1862, when the Mexican army defeated the much larger French forces
in the city of Puebla. Piñatas, mariachi music and, of course, Mexican foods add
to the Cinco de Mayo festivities, which are almost exclusively celebrated in the
Southwestern United States and virtually ignored in Mexico.

tortilla soup

LEE COCHRAN

Don't let the long list of ingredients fool you...this is simple and delicious!

1 large onion, chopped
1 jalapeño, seeded and chopped
3 cloves garlic, chopped
1 tablespoon olive oil
1 can (14.5 ounces) stewed tomatoes
2 cups beef broth
2 cups chicken broth
1 can (10.75 ounces) condensed tomato soup
1-1/2 cups water
2 teaspoons Worcestershire sauce
1 teaspoon ground cumin
1/4 to 1/2 teaspoon chili powder
6 corn tortillas, cut into thin strips
2 avocados, chopped
1 cup (4 ounces) shredded sharp
   cheddar cheese
1 cup shredded cooked chicken
1/2 cup chopped green onions
Sour cream and cilantro

In a large saucepan, sauté onion, jalapeño and garlic in oil. Add the tomatoes, broth, soup, water, Worcestershire sauce, cumin and chili powder; simmer for 1 hour. Bake tortilla strips at 350° for 5 minutes or until crispy. In soup bowls, place avocados, cheese, chicken and green onions; ladle soup into bowls. Garnish with crisp tortilla strips, sour cream and cilantro.

SERVES 6-8

beef and pork tamales

PAULE JOHNSTON

Based on 15 pounds of meat, roast twice as much beef as pork. The meat can be made in advance; simmer and reseason the day before you plan to make the tamales (meat should be cool). I collect my own meat fat and drippings to use for lard. Beating the lard and bacon grease until fluffy takes time. I trade off beating with whoever is helping me. Light masa is the secret to good homemade tamales!

Bottom round *or* rump roast beef and
   pork butt (ratio: 2 beef to 1 pork)
2 to 3 large onions, sliced
1 large green pepper, chopped
3 bay leaves
2 to 3 tablespoons dried oregano
Minced garlic, salt and pepper to taste

sauce:

3 tablespoons dried oregano
2 tablespoons ground cumin
3 to 4 bay leaves
Juice of 3 lemons
2 cans (28 ounces *each*) red chile sauce
2 jars chili paste, rinsed out with red wine
Minced garlic to taste

Onion juice and Worcestershire
   sauce, optional
Salt, cayenne and other seasonings of
   cook's choice

tamales:

2 pounds bacon grease
1 pound lard
10 pounds masa
6 to 7 tablespoons salt
4 tablespoons baking powder
4 tablespoons chili powder
1 large package of corn husks
2 to 3 cans (4 ounces *each*) whole green
   chiles, sliced lengthwise
1 block of longhorn cheese, cut into strips

Place meat in a covered roaster. Top with onions, green pepper, bay leaves, oregano, garlic, salt and pepper. Cover and roast at 250° overnight (with vents, if any, closed). Pour off drippings; discard seasonings if visible, and fat and bone if you have it. Shred the meat and put in a large stovetop pot.

The day before you make the tamales, add the sauce ingredients to the pot with the meat. Simmer slowly, stirring often, tasting and adding seasonings as needed. Make it hotter than you think you want it, as steaming and freezing removes the heat and flavor.

To make the tamales: In a very large mixing bowl, beat bacon grease and lard until very light and fluffy, like whipping cream. Beat in the masa, salt, baking powder and chili powder. Keep beating until a "dab of masa" rises to the top when dropped in a glass of cold water. Taste to be sure it's salty enough. Meanwhile, clean silk from dry corn husks. Soak husks in warm water to make pliable. Spread a thin layer of masa on the top two-thirds of a drained husk (wide end is the top). Add meat in the middle, not too thick. Add a strip of green chile and cheese. Fold in one side, then fold the other over the center meat section; fold bottom (empty) pointed section up and dab with masa to hold it together.

Stand up finished tamales in a steamer; steam gently until masa pulls away from the husk, close to an hour. Steam tamales of like size together. Remove from steamer and lay flat on wire racks to cool. Eat or freeze.

chicken enchiladas

BETTY DAVIS

1/4 cup butter
1/4 cup all-purpose flour
3 cups chicken broth
1 tablespoon ground cumin
1 teaspoon salt
1/2 teaspoon pepper
1 cup (8 ounces) sour cream
2 tablespoons chopped jalapeños
1 onion, chopped
1 green pepper, chopped
1 tablespoon oil
4 chicken breasts, cooked and cubed
12 flour tortillas
3 cups (12 ounces) shredded
   Monterey Jack cheese

Preheat oven to 350°. In a saucepan, melt butter; stir in flour and cook for 1 minute. Add broth, cumin, salt and pepper; mix well. Remove from the heat; stir in sour cream and jalapeños. Set aside. In a skillet, sauté onion and green pepper in oil until soft. Add cooked chicken. Spoon onto tortillas and roll up; place seam side down in a glass baking dish. Cover with sauce and cheese. Bake for 30 minutes or until bubbly and browned.

SERVES 4-6

corn cazuela

MARGARET GRIFFITH

A casserole named for the earthenware dish in which it is traditionally cooked. This one is lined with corn husks.

12 ears of corn with husks
3 fresh Anaheim chiles
1 cup butter, softened
3/4 cup fine yellow cornmeal
1/4 cup sugar
1 package (3 ounces) cream cheese, softened
1 teaspoon salt
1/3 cup heavy cream
2 cups (8 ounces) shredded
   Monterey Jack cheese

Remove husks from corn. Soak wide outer husks in boiling water until softened, about 15 minutes. Meanwhile, roast the chiles; peel, seed and cut into 1-inch squares or strips. Drain the corn husks well. Line a 13-inch x 9-inch x 2-inch baking dish with husks, overlapping if necessary and allowing excess to hang over the sides. Cut corn from cobs. Set aside 1 cup; purée remainder in batches in a food processor.

Preheat oven to 375°. In a large mixing bowl, beat butter until fluffy. Beat in cornmeal, sugar, cream cheese and salt. Stir in reserved corn and corn purée. Blend in cream. Pour half of the corn mixture into prepared dish; smooth the top but do not spread to edges of husks. Cover with cheese and roasted chiles. Top with remaining corn mixture. Fold husks over to partially cover mixture. Cover and bake for 1 hour. Uncover and let stand for 20 minutes before serving. Cazuela will firm as it cools.

SERVES 8-10

rice and chile casserole

MARGARET GRIFFITH

6 cups cooked white rice
12 poblano chiles
1/2 cup corn oil
7 cloves garlic, *divided*
2 large white onions, sliced diagonally
6 large ripe tomatoes
1 medium white onion, quartered
Salt and pepper to taste

cream:

2 cups crème fraîche *or* 1 cup heavy cream
  whisked with 1 cup sour cream
2 cups plain yogurt
1/2 teaspoon salt
1/2 teaspoon freshly ground pepper
2 cloves garlic, minced

topping:

5 egg whites
1/4 teaspoon salt
4 egg yolks, lightly beaten
2-1/2 cups shredded mozzarella *or* Oaxaca
2 cups shredded Monterey Jack *or* Gruyère

Set the cooked rice aside. Roast the chiles; peel and seed, then soak in salted water for 20 minutes to remove piquancy. Cut into strips. Heat oil in a saucepan; brown 4 garlic cloves, then remove and discard. Sauté onion slices in the same oil until transparent. Stir in chile strips; cook 5 more minutes.

In a blender or food processor, grind the tomatoes with the raw onion and remaining garlic cloves; strain. Add tomato mixture to sautéed chile mixture. Season with salt and pepper. Cook over low heat for 30 minutes or until sauce thickens. Meanwhile, stir together cream and yogurt. Season with salt, pepper and garlic; set aside. In a small mixing bowl, beat egg whites with salt until stiff. Then carefully fold in egg yolks.

Preheat oven to 350°. Spoon half of the rice into a deep buttered baking dish. Cover with half of the tomato-chile sauce and half of the cream mixture; sprinkle with half of the cheeses. Top with remaining rice, tomato-chile sauce, cream and cheeses. Spread egg topping over the casserole. Bake for 45 minutes or until topping is golden brown. Serve immediately.

SERVES 8-12

stuffed poblanos—
baked chile rellenos

MARGARET GRIFFITH

Homegrown flowers are the best, but if you must buy them, be sure to look at the lower ends of the stems: If they are freshly cut and the foliage looks good, then it is a good buy; otherwise make another selection.

3 poblano chiles, halved lengthwise
 and seeded
3/4 cup corn kernels
1/4 cup chopped red onion
1/4 cup chopped celery
1/4 cup chopped red bell pepper
1/4 cup chopped fresh parsley
3/4 cup shredded sharp cheddar cheese
1 jalapeño, seeded and minced
1 tablespoon bread crumbs
1/2 teaspoon salt
Pepper to taste
Sour cream *or* crème fraîche

Preheat oven to 375°. Place poblano halves on a lightly oiled baking sheet. In a bowl, combine the corn, onion, celery, red pepper, parsley, cheese, jalapeño, bread crumbs, salt and pepper; toss thoroughly. Stuff into the poblanos. Bake for 30 minutes or until bubbly. Serve immediately with sour cream on top.

SERVES 2-3 AS AN ENTRÉE OR
6 AS A FIRST COURSE

tres leches cake

This traditional Mexican cake translates as "three milks."

1/2 cup unsalted butter, softened
I cup sugar
5 eggs
I to 2 teaspoons vanilla extract, *divided*
1-1/2 cups all-purpose flour
1-1/2 teaspoons baking powder
I can (14 ounces) sweetened condensed milk
I can (12 ounces) evaporated milk
I cup goat's milk *or* whole milk
1-1/2 cups heavy cream
1/4 cup powdered sugar

Preheat oven to 350°. Grease and flour a 13-inch x 9-inch x 2-inch baking dish. With a mixer, beat butter and sugar at medium speed until fluffy; mix in eggs and 1/2 teaspoon vanilla. Combine flour and baking powder; add gradually to butter mixture, stirring to blend. Pour into prepared pan. Bake for 30 minutes or until a toothpick inserted in center comes out clean. Pierce cake with a fork all over. Combine the three milks and pour over cake. Cool to room temperature. Cover and refrigerate until well chilled, at least 4 hours or overnight.

With a mixer, beat cream, powdered sugar and remaining vanilla at medium-high speed until thick; spread over cake. Serve chilled with whipped cream, melted chocolate, or dulce de leche or cinnamon ice cream.

SERVES 15

MOTHER'S DAY

It is traditional in the South to cook breakfast for your mother on the day devoted to moms—the second Sunday in May—since the rest of the year, she's the person who plans, prepares or sends out for your meals. We've included some brunch items, as we assume the lady of the house may want to sleep in.

northern ireland's best currant scones

KAREN TERRELL

This recipe is from Allison Schoenbeck's Northern Irish mother. As with biscuits, scones are lightest when the dough is handled minimally.

2 cups all-purpose flour
1-1/2 tablespoons baking powder
1/2 teaspoon salt
1/4 cup cold butter
1 to 2 tablespoons sugar
1/3 cup currants
Pinch of lemon *or* orange zest, optional
3/4 to 1 cup milk, room temperature

Preheat oven to 450°. Sift flour, baking powder and salt into a bowl; cut in butter. Add sugar, currants and lemon zest if desired. Pour in about 3/4 cup milk and stir with a wooden spoon until it forms a soft dough; if the dough is too crumbly, add more milk, just until dough forms a ball. Pick up and knead no more than 1 minute.

Roll out 1 inch thick on a floured surface. Place in a cake pan, pat gently to fit and score with a knife. Or cut with a small biscuit cutter and place on an ungreased cookie sheet. Brush lightly with milk or egg, then sprinkle sugar on top. Bake for 10-15 minutes or until light golden brown. Watch so they don't overbake!

MAKES 1 DOZEN MEDIUM OR
2 DOZEN SMALL SCONES

eggs dartmouth

NORA WATSON

*This easy homemade tomato sauce has infinite
uses and also freezes well.*

nora's tomato sauce:

2 pounds fresh ripe tomatoes
1 medium onion, quartered
5 tablespoons butter
Salt to taste

Blanch the tomatoes for 1 minute in boiling
water. Peel and cut into coarse pieces. In a
saucepan, sauté the onion in butter until
translucent, not browned. Add tomatoes.
Cook, uncovered, at a very slow simmer for
45 minutes. Discard onion pieces. Stir and
mash large pieces of tomato. Taste and
correct the salt. Use immediately in Eggs
Dartmouth recipe, or refrigerate or freeze
for another use.

eggs dartmouth:

2 eggs per person
Chicken broth for poaching
Nora's Tomato Sauce (recipe at left)
1 English muffin per person,
    split and toasted
2 slices sharp cheddar cheese per person
Watercress for garnish

Poach eggs in 1 cup chicken broth with 1/2
cup of tomato sauce. Place eggs on English
muffin halves; top with cheese. Spoon hot
tomato sauce over egg and cheese. Garnish
with watercress.

COMFORT FOOD

For those times when a friend is recuperating or a family has lost a loved one, making a comforting casserole, salad or dessert for them is one way to show you care.

anna beth's sausage casserole

DANA PARKEY

A nice change from the typical "get well" casserole. For the sausage, I use Jimmy Dean or Owens. This makes a lot and it freezes well.

1 pound hot bulk sausage
1 pound mild bulk sausage
2-1/2 cups sliced celery
1 cup chopped green bell pepper
3/4 cup chopped onion
4 tablespoons slivered almonds, *divided*
4-1/2 cups water

2 envelopes Lipton chicken noodle soup mix
1 cup uncooked long-grain rice
1/2 teaspoon salt
1/4 cup butter

Preheat oven to 350°. Crumble the sausage into a large skillet and cook until browned; drain. Add celery, green pepper and onion; cook until veggies are tender. Add 3 tablespoons almonds. In another pan, bring water to a boil. Add soup mix and rice; simmer for 20 minutes. Combine meat and rice mixtures. Spoon into a greased 13-inch x 9-inch x 2-inch baking pan or three round foil pans. Sprinkle with remaining almonds. Bake for 1 hour.

penny's funeral pasta salad

DORIS HEARD

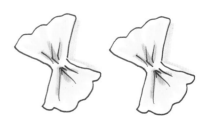

My friend Penny is great about taking food over to families who will have lots of guests coming over after funeral services. Everyone loves it, and it holds up well over a period of time. Easy to make, it serves many and travels well when the occasion arises.

1 box (16 ounces) farfalle
3 cups thinly sliced spinach
1 cup kalamata olives
1/2 cup chopped sun-dried tomatoes
1/4 cup chopped red onion
1 package (4 ounces) crumbed feta cheese

dressing:

1/2 cup olive oil
3 tablespoons red wine vinegar
1 clove garlic, crushed
1/2 teaspoon salt
1/2 teaspoon pepper

Cook pasta according to package directions; drain and rinse in cold water. Place in a large bowl; add the spinach, olives, tomatoes, onion and feta cheese. Blend dressing ingredients well by whisking or shaking. Pour over the salad and toss gently. Refrigerate until serving.

SERVES 8-10

Keep fresh greens or foliage in the kitchen. Herbs smell good and come in infinite shades of green. Besides being handy, keeping herbs and greens around as décor brings the outdoors in. An attractive pitcher or glass will do for a vase. Lime sweet potato vine is a beautiful choice.

anne's ham and spinach roll-ups

DANA PARKEY

1 can (10.75 ounces) condensed
    cream of celery soup
1 cup (8 ounces) sour cream
2 tablespoons Dijon mustard
1 cup uncooked instant rice
1 package (10 ounces) frozen spinach,
    thawed and drained
1 cup (8 ounces) small-curd cottage cheese
2 eggs, lightly beaten
1/2 cup finely chopped onion
1/4 cup all-purpose flour
18 slices cooked ham, thinly sliced (long
    pieces work best)
2 cups bread crumbs
3 tablespoons butter
Parsley and paprika for garnish

Preheat oven to 350°. In a bowl, mix
together the soup, sour cream and mustard.
Transfer half of the mixture to another bowl;
add the rice, spinach, cottage cheese, eggs,
onion and flour. Mix well. Place 2 heaping
tablespoons of spinach mixture on each ham
slice. Roll up and place seam side down in an
11-inch x 7-inch x 2-inch baking dish.
Spread the remaining soup mixture on top.

Bake for 30-35 minutes. Let stand for 5-10
minutes. Brown bread crumbs in butter;
sprinkle over roll-ups. Garnish with parsley
and paprika.

SERVES 6-9

chocolate chess pie

1-1/2 cups sugar
3-1/2 tablespoons baking cocoa
1/4 cup butter, melted
2 eggs, beaten
1 can (5 ounces) evaporated milk
1/2 teaspoon vanilla extract
1 unbaked pastry shell

Preheat oven to 350°. Combine the first
six ingredients; pour into pie shell. Bake
for 45 minutes. Cool on a wire rack.

SERVES 6-8

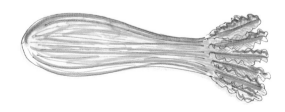

star-spangled
summer

star-spangled *Summer*

Summer brings memories of enjoying fresh tomatoes, corn on the cob, seafood, cooling dishes and curried dishes, which have a cooling effect. We cook outside or on the stovetop and keep the ovens off. Quick, cool and easy are the bywords of the season.

It's a fun and festive time of year, with weddings, picnics and summer vacations on the calendar…and, of course, Independence Day celebrations. So we've collected recipes for hosting a bridal luncheon, down-home foods for the Fourth and French specialties for Bastille Day. With our exotic menus and spa day treatments, you can enjoy a vacation without leaving the comfort of home!

In the garden, it's necessary to water during the cooler hours and to water deeply for plants' roots. Be sure to water new plantings well, and add mulch to keep in moisture. Work outdoors early in the morning or later in the evening. Pinch back annuals and perennials to encourage new growth. Herbs, with their subtle summer flavors, are particularly welcome now. It is time to plant basil, mint, rosemary, eggplant, okra, sweet potato and—if you have the room—watermelon.

Our native plants that love heat and humidity, and don't need much water, were eco-friendly long before we knew what eco-friendly meant! They are very low-maintenance but may get too comfortable and prosper too well. These plants include: angel's trumpet, aspidistra, bamboo (try to find clumping bamboo), bignonia vine, canna lilies, Cherokee roses, chrysanthemum, clematis, Confederate jasmine, coreopsis, crinum lilies, cycads, datura, equisetum, fig vine, hibiscus, holly fern, Lady Banks roses, lantana, oleander, ornamental peppers, Persian shield, shrimp plant, sword fern, verbena, vinca and zinnia.

Quick, cool and easy are the bywords of summer.

While some plants love heat, even the hardiest among us look for ways to cool down, especially during the dog days of summer. Here are some hints to beat the heat:

* Freeze mint or edible flowers in ice cubes or ring molds to keep beverages cold and look pretty at the same time!

* Enjoy refreshing beverages such as a Ramos gin fizz, Pimm's Cup, cocktails made with Brazilian cachaça; Prosecco, a dry sparkling wine from Italy that's wonderful with straw berries; and other lighter wines like Pinot Grigio (Pinot Gris) and Rosé.

* Use scented geraniums to garnish drinks. Lavender is wonderful with club soda and a dash of lemon, and it is equally tasty in a glass of Champagne.

* Garnish dishes with cool greens: mint, cilantro and basil. Sprinkle edible flowers over salads for a tasty, nutritious and creative touch.

* Float rose petals or other flowers in a punch bowl or clear glass bowl as a centerpiece for a summer party. Or float them in the pool.

* Turn fresh summer fruit into a delightful dessert. Add your choice of fruit to vanilla ice cream; chop peeled green stem ginger, mint leaves or lavender and sprinkle it over the fruit for a wonderful new flavor.

* Take a cooling bath; add rosemary, mint, scented geranium or lavender to tepid bath water. Place cucumber slices over your eyes for a refresher. See other tips in Spa Day (page 256).

* Place a scented flower in a small vase on your nightstand for a fresh breath of summer as you turn in and wake up.

BRIDAL LUNCHEONS

Here comes the bride…to a brunch or lunch in her honor! Tea sandwiches,
chicken and shrimp salads, aspics, homemade ice cream and real flowers
decorating a cake are the order of the day. For additional salad selections,
see the Bulb and Plant Mart section, starting on page 36.

cucumber tea sandwiches

ADRIENNE BULLARD

1/2 cup rice wine vinegar
1/2 cup water
1/2 teaspoon salt
6 green onion tops, chopped
1 cucumber, sliced into thin rounds
1 loaf of white *or* whole-wheat bread,
   sliced into thin rounds
Unsalted butter

Combine vinegar, water and salt in a bowl;
add the green onion tops and cucumber
rounds. Let stand for 1 hour or more.
Drain off liquid and pat dry. Spread one
side of each bread round with butter;
place several cucumber slices on half of
the buttered bread, then top with remaining
buttered bread.

MAKES 16 SANDWICHES

jerry's molded salad
LINEY ROTAN

This is a fabulous aspic…great with barbecued chicken, beef or pork. Depending on what you're serving it with, fill the "hole" in the mold with sliced avocados or chicken salad.

1 package (3 ounces) lemon gelatin
1 cup boiling water
1 can (8 ounces) crushed pineapple, drained
1 can (8 ounces) tomato sauce
8 green onion tops, diced
3/4 to 1 cup diced celery
1 good shot of Worcestershire sauce
Cracked pepper to taste
Mayonnaise

In a bowl, dissolve gelatin in boiling water. Stir in the pineapple, tomato sauce, green onion tops, celery, Worcestershire sauce and pepper. Grease a ring mold with mayonnaise; add gelatin mixture. Chill until set. Top each slice with a touch of mayonnaise.

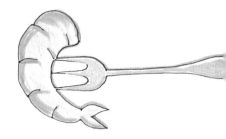

shrimp luncheon salad
CAROLYN DAVIS

1 can (15 ounces) shrimp soup
2 tablespoons unflavored gelatin
1/2 cup cold water
2 cups cooked salad shrimp
1/2 cup chopped green onions
1 package (8 ounces) cream cheese, cubed
1 cup mayonnaise
1 cup chopped celery
1 tablespoon lemon juice
Lettuce and additional mayonnaise

Heat soup. Dissolve gelatin in cold water and add to soup. Add the remaining ingredients and mix thoroughly. Pour into a greased mold. Refrigerate. Just before serving, unmold onto a platter; surround with lettuce and serve with mayonnaise.

SERVES 8

chicken with avocado salad dressing

This recipe originated with Mariquita Masterson and was given to Ann Kelsey by Anita Stude during the summer of 1998 in Weimar, Texas. Now it's yours to share!

6 whole chicken breasts
1 bunch cilantro, *divided*
1 tomato, chopped
1 green bell pepper, chopped
2 white onions, chopped, *divided*
Salt and cracked black pepper to taste
Olive oil, lemon juice and chicken
  broth for dressing
3 avocados, chopped
Lettuce cups, fruit and vegetables for garnish

Poach the chicken breasts in enough water to cover, adding 12 stems of cilantro, tomato, green pepper, half of the chopped onions, salt and pepper. Cook just long enough for the chicken to be cooked, about 15-20 minutes. Let the chicken cool in its broth. Meanwhile, chop a clump of cilantro; set aside. Make a dressing of olive oil, lemon juice and chicken broth; season with salt and pepper.

Remove the chicken from its broth; remove the skin and cut meat into bite-size pieces. One hour before serving, mix two-thirds of the dressing with the chicken, chopped cilantro and onions; mix the remaining dressing separately with the chopped avocados. Right before serving, strain the avocados and add them to the chicken salad. Spoon into lettuce cups; garnish with fruit and vegetables you have on hand.

SERVES 6-8

lemon cake

MEG TAPP

Served with lemon ice cream, this is a refreshingly tart dessert.

1 box (18.25 ounces) lemon cake mix
1 box (3.4 ounces) lemon pudding mix
1-1/4 cups water
1/3 cup oil
4 eggs

icing:

1-1/2 cups powdered sugar
Juice of 1 lemon
Grated zest of 1 lemon, optional

Preheat oven to 350°. Using a mixer, beat the cake mix, pudding mix, water, oil and eggs on low speed until combined. Then beat on high for 2 minutes. Pour into a greased and floured Bundt pan. Bake for 45-55 minutes or until a toothpick comes out clean. Cool in the pan for 10 minutes, then turn cake out onto a wire rack to cool.

Put powdered sugar in a mixer bowl. Heat lemon juice to a boil. Slowly add hot lemon juice to powdered sugar, beating on medium speed. Add zest if desired. You may not need all of the lemon juice, so check the consistency of the icing as you go (the icing is the right consistency when you can spoon it out of the mixing bowl with a spoon and not have icing drip off the bottom of the spoon). Drizzle icing over cake; it will harden a little when it hits the cooled cake.

SERVES 12-16

lemon ice cream

ROBIN HOWELL

3 tablespoons lemon juice
2 teaspoons grated lemon peel
1 cup sugar
2 cups light cream *or* half-and-half
1/8 teaspoon salt

Prepare your ice cream maker. Combine lemon juice, peel and sugar; mix well. Stir in cream and salt. Freeze in an ice cream freezer. You can double or triple the recipe, but use slightly less sugar (about 1-1/2 cups for double and about the same amount of salt).

MAKES 3 CUPS

lime and lemon posset

ELLEN MORRIS

"Posset" refers to an old English drink made similarly to this simple pudding. This recipe delivers great results with very little effort. It's a lovely light dessert served with a little cookie on the side.

2-1/4 cups heavy cream
3/4 cup plus 1 teaspoon sugar, *divided*
3 tablespoons lemon juice
2 tablespoons lime juice
1 teaspoon grated lemon peel
1 teaspoon grated lime peel

In a saucepan, bring cream and 3/4 cup sugar to a boil over medium-high heat, stirring until sugar dissolves. Boil for 3 minutes, stirring constantly, and adjusting heat as needed to prevent mixture from boiling over. Remove from the heat. Stir in lemon and lime juices; cool for 10 minutes. Stir mixture again and divide among six 1/2-cup ramekins, favorite small bowls or demitasse cups. Cover and chill until set, 4 hours or overnight. Mix lemon peel, lime peel and remaining sugar; sprinkle on top of possets before serving.

SERVES 6

fruit dip

A cooling summer treat!

1 package (8 ounces) cream cheese, softened
1 jar (7 ounces) marshmallow creme
1/8 teaspoon ground ginger
Fresh fruit of your choice

In a small bowl, combine the cream cheese,
marshmallow creme and ginger until smooth.
Arrange fruit on a pretty platter with the
bowl of dip in the center, garnished with
fresh ginger, mint or basil leaves. If serving
fresh pineapple, save the top for the center
of the platter and serve the dip on the side.

FOURTH OF JULY

*The Fourth of July is our big summer celebration. Picnics and outings and
a trip to the bay or ranch are special for family gatherings.*

South Texas Fourth of July ~ Rose Cullen, Katie Cullen, Kathy McCord

*Our large family gathers for all special holidays at
our Buena Vista Ranch, which is situated on a point
of land on Laguna Madre, just across from South
Padre Island. The cool winds keep us comfortable for
the Fourth of July, when the family gathers to watch
the fireworks from the Island. Rose developed these
recipes, which are prepared by the "tres Marias" in
the kitchen, who add to the menu by making fresh
salsa and pico de gallo. The crab enchiladas are a
special treat with fresh crabmeat from the Gulf. We
also enjoy empanadas, and for dessert, chocolate
chip and oatmeal raisin cookies.*

favorite empanadas

3 packages (3 ounces *each*) cream cheese,
  softened
1/2 cup butter, softened
1-1/2 cups all-purpose flour

filling:

1/2 medium onion, chopped
2 tablespoons oil
1/2 pound ground beef
1/2 pound ground sausage
1/4 cup small raisins
1/4 cup slivered almonds
1 can (8 ounces) tomato sauce
1 egg
Few drops of ice water

To make the dough: Blend cream cheese and
butter; add flour. Form into a soft ball. Wrap
in waxed paper and refrigerate for 1 hour.

Preheat oven to 350°. In a large skillet,
sauté onion in oil until clear. Add beef and
sausage; cook until browned. Stir in raisins,
almonds and tomato sauce; set aside. Take
ball of dough out of refrigerator. Roll out
flat; use a biscuit cutter to cut round circles.
Put a spoonful of meat mixture on each
dough circle and fold over. Press edges with
a fork to seal. Beat egg with ice water; brush
over empanadas. Place on baking sheets. Bake
for 10-12 minutes or until golden brown.

MAKES 3 DOZEN

Wine Recommendation: for red, Malbec,
Messina Hof Pinot Noir or another light red…
for white, Sauvignon Blanc

crab or chicken enchiladas

1 medium onion, finely chopped
1 medium green pepper, finely chopped
5 tablespoons canola oil, *divided*
1/2 pound cooked crabmeat *or* 3 chicken
  breasts, poached and cubed
1/4 cup butter
2 tablespoons all-purpose flour
1/2 teaspoon salt
2 cups milk *or* half-and-half cream
1/2 pound Velveeta cheese, cubed
1 jar (4 ounces) diced pimientos, drained
12 corn tortillas
1-1/2 cups (6 ounces) shredded cheddar
  cheese, *divided*

Sauté onion and green pepper in 1 tablespoon oil. Add crab or chicken; stir and set aside. In a saucepan, melt butter; add flour and blend well. Add salt and milk; cook until thickened, about 5-6 minutes. Add Velveeta; cook until melted. Add pimientos. Set the sauce aside and prepare the tortillas.

Preheat oven to 350°. Heat the remaining oil in a small skillet. Add tortillas to oil, one at a time, to soften. Remove and blot on paper towels. Place crab (or chicken) mixture on each tortilla; top with 1/2 tablespoon shredded cheddar. Roll up firmly and place seam side down in a 13-inch x 9-inch x 2-inch glass baking dish. Pour sauce over enchiladas. Sprinkle with remaining cheddar. (Can make a day ahead to this point.) Bake, uncovered, for 25 minutes or until bubbly and golden brown. Serve with salsa and pico de gallo.

ranch salsa

5 medium tomatoes, chopped
1 medium onion, chopped
2 small Serranos *or* jalapeños, seeded and
   chopped (or more to taste)
1 tablespoon canola oil
Handful of cilantro, chopped
Salt to taste

Combine all ingredients in a saucepan and
cook until blended. Serve salsa warm over
scrambled eggs, fried-basted eggs or grilled
fish, or as a dip for empanadas.

chocolate chip cookies

1 cup butter, softened
3/4 cup sugar
3/4 cup packed brown sugar
1 teaspoon vanilla extract
2 eggs
2-1/4 cups all-purpose flour
1 teaspoon baking soda
1/4 teaspoon salt
2 cups (12 ounces) semisweet chocolate chips
1 cup pecan halves

Preheat oven to 375°. With a mixer, beat the
butter, sugars and vanilla until creamy. Add
eggs, one at a time, beating after each addition. Combine the flour, baking soda and
salt; gradually beat into creamed mixture.
Stir in chocolate chips. Drop by rounded
teaspoonfuls onto ungreased cookie sheets;
press a pecan half on top of each. Bake for
9-11 minutes.

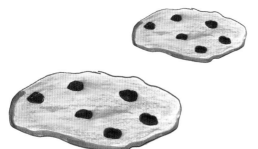
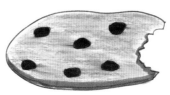

oatmeal raisin cookies

1 cup butter, softened
1 cup packed brown sugar
1/2 cup sugar
2 eggs
1 teaspoon vanilla extract
1-1/2 cups all-purpose flour
1 teaspoon baking soda
1 teaspoon ground cinnamon
1/4 to 1/2 teaspoon salt
3 cups quick-cooking *or* old-fashioned oats
1 cup raisins

Preheat oven to 350°. With a mixer, beat the butter and sugars until creamy. Add eggs and vanilla; beat well. Combine the flour, baking soda, cinnamon and salt; add to creamed mixture and mix well. Stir in oats and raisins. Drop by rounded tablespoonfuls onto ungreased cookie sheets. Bake for 10-12 minutes or until golden brown. Cool for 1 minute before removing to wire racks.

MAKES ABOUT 4 DOZEN

ab's shrimp boil
SIDNEY FAY

My husband, Ab, and I gather friends at our Texas Corinthian Yacht Club home for a Summer Shrimp Boil. Ab prepares the shrimp while I prepare the side dishes. It is no frills—the tables are covered with newspaper (comic sections for color)....paper towels serve as napkins...butter for corn on the cob is melted and poured into a painter's pan for "rolling" an ear of corn. We also serve plain white bread and salads, although it seems no one ever eats the salads! Get the shrimp with the heads on...if your guests can't handle that, don't invite them!

4 bags of crab boil
3 to 4 heaping handfuls of rock salt
1/4 bottle of Worcestershire sauce
10 good shakes of Tabasco
3 lemons
1 pound of shrimp per person

Fill a large pot three-quarters full with water; bring to a boil. Add the crab boil, rock salt, Worcestershire sauce and Tabasco; squeeze the lemon juice in and then toss the lemons. Add the shrimp; remove from the heat the second they turn pink.

corn on the cob with honey

MIMI KERR

Corn is so sweet when freshly picked. However, most of us can't have it straight from the field, so adding honey to the water helps restore nature's sweetness.

6 ears fresh sweet corn (preferably white)
1/3 cup honey
1/2 cup butter, melted
1/2 teaspoon salt
1/4 teaspoon pepper

Shuck and silk the corn and cut away any blemished areas. Bring a large pot of water to a boil, adding the honey. Add corn; after water comes back to a boil, cook for about 8 minutes. In a baking dish long enough to hold an ear of corn, stir together the butter, salt and pepper. Drain the corn; roll in butter mixture and serve immediately.

SERVES 6

cathy's potato salad

MIMI KERR

4 large baking potatoes
2 cups diced celery
3/4 pound bacon, cooked and crumbled
1 cup mayonnaise
Salt and freshly ground pepper to taste
2 tablespoons thinly sliced green onions

Peel potatoes and cut in half widthwise. Place in a large pot of salted water; bring to a boil. Simmer for 20 minutes or until tender when pierced with a fork; drain. Dice warm potatoes into small chunks and place in a large bowl. Add the celery and bacon; gently toss with mayonnaise (mix well, but leave potatoes chunky). Season generously with salt and pepper. Add more mayonnaise if desired. Spoon into a serving dish and refrigerate. Before serving, sprinkle with green onions.

SERVES 6

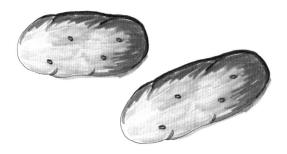

farm dinner salad

GAIL HENDRYX

Serve this hearty summertime salad with flavorful bread.

2/3 cup olive oil

4 to 5 cloves garlic, minced

1 teaspoon kosher *or* smoked salt

Ground pepper

2 zucchini, cut lengthwise into
    1/4-inch slices

2 yellow summer squash, cut lengthwise into
    1/4-inch slices

2 medium sweet onions, cut into
    1/2-inch slices

1 red bell pepper, sliced

1 small package of baby carrots

1 ear of corn, kernels removed

1 cup green beans, simmered in salted water
    until tender

1 cup edamame, cooked in salted water

4 to 8 turkey *or* other sausage links (not
    breakfast sausage)

4 to 6 cups baby greens

Turn on broiler. Line a large jelly-roll pan with foil. In a bowl, mix oil, garlic, salt and pepper. Dip zucchini and yellow squash slices in the oil mixture and place on prepared pan. Put under the broiler until tender and a bit caramelized. Remove and put the squash in a pile at the edge of a very large serving platter. Pour any juices into a cup. Repeat with onions, red pepper, carrots and corn, putting each veggie in a different stack. (Add more oil, garlic, salt and pepper to bowl if necessary.) Put the green beans and edamame in separate piles around edge of platter. While vegetables are broiling, grill sausages.

If there is any remaining marinade and it is not too salty, use it as a base for vinaigrette, adding cider or wine vinegar. Or mix buttermilk with lemon juice, a little olive oil, salt and pepper for a dressing. Toss with the baby greens and put in the center of the platter. Top with sausages. Each diner makes their own salad from the bounty presented.

SERVES 4-6

Variation: Use whatever vegetables you like. If you prefer raw veggies, use the zucchini, yellow squash and blanched green beans, and add radishes and cucumbers. Exchange the sausages for a white flaky fish. Season the fish with salt and pepper; dip it in egg white and then chopped soft herbs and sauté in olive oil.

Wine Recommendation: a light red such as Llano Estacado Shiraz, Beaujolais or Spanish Grenache

ranch dressing

1/4 cup mayonnaise
1/4 cup buttermilk
2 teaspoons sugar
1/2 teaspoon vinegar
1/4 teaspoon garlic powder
1/4 teaspoon minced fresh dill
1/4 teaspoon minced fresh parsley
1/8 teaspoon onion powder
1/8 teaspoon salt
Dash of paprika

In a small bowl, whisk all ingredients until combined. Serve with your favorite lettuce salad or as a dip for veggies.

frances' mint dressing

DANA PARKEY

3 tablespoons coarsely chopped fresh mint
2 tablespoons chopped onion
3/4 cup sugar
1 teaspoon dry mustard
1 teaspoon salt
1/3 cup cider vinegar
1 cup vegetable oil

Pulse mint and onion in a blender or food processor. Add sugar, mustard, salt and vinegar; blend on high. With blender going, add oil very slowly, blending until thick. Refrigerate. Serve on fruit salad.

MAKES ABOUT 2 CUPS

"Weather means more when you have a garden. There's nothing like listening to a shower and thinking how it is soaking in around your green beans."

~Marcelene Cox, 20th-century American writer

all-star apple pie

MEG TAPP

Covered with pastry stars, this beautiful pie charms the adults and thrills the kids!

1 refrigerated pie crust
1/2 cup butter, softened
1/4 cup sugar
1 egg
1 teaspoon vanilla *or* lemon extract
1 tablespoon milk
1-1/2 cups all-purpose flour
1/4 teaspoon baking powder
Pinch of salt

filling:

3/4 cup sugar
1-1/2 tablespoons all-purpose flour
1 teaspoon ground cinnamon
1/2 teaspoon salt
1/2 teaspoon ground nutmeg
Pinch of allspice, optional
6 to 8 Granny Smith apples
Lemon juice
2 tablespoons butter

Take one roll of pie crust from package (to use for bottom crust) and leave at room temperature while making the pastry (for top of pie) and filling. With a mixer, cream the butter. Gradually add sugar and beat until light in texture. Add egg, vanilla and milk all at once and beat thoroughly. Combine the flour, baking powder and salt; add to creamed mixture and blend well. Refrigerate while making the filling.

In a large bowl, mix the sugar, flour, cinnamon, salt, nutmeg and allspice if desired. Peel, core and slice the apples. (If they start to turn brown, sprinkle with a tiny bit of lemon juice.) Add apples to dry ingredients and toss; set aside. On a floured surface, roll out dough 1/4 to 1/2 inch thick. (If dough is too sticky, add more flour.) Using a star-shaped cookie cutter (or more than one cutter of varying sizes), cut out as many stars as possible.

Preheat oven to 425°. Line pie plate with ready-made pie crust sheet. Mound filling into crust. Dot with butter; sprinkle with lemon juice. Cover the top of the pie with pastry stars (they will overlap). If top or bottom crust is hanging over the edge of the pie plate, pinch it back in toward the filling. Sprinkle lightly with sugar if desired. Bake for 10 minutes. Reduce heat to 350°; bake for 30–40 minutes (check at 20 minutes; if it's getting too brown, cover loosely with foil). Store at room temperature for up to 24 hours. After that, refrigerate.

Variation: Use the cookie cutter to make cheese stars to melt over the top. Or serve with Vanilla Ice Cream (recipe below) with 1/2 teaspoon of cinnamon added.

vanilla ice cream

MOLLIE PETTIGREW

*Very easy—no cooking! You can add cinnamon
or fresh peaches or strawberries if you like.*

5 eggs, *separated*
1-3/4 cups sugar
Milk to fill (about 3/4 gallon)
3 to 4 teaspoons vanilla extract
1-1/2 pints heavy cream, whipped

Prepare your ice cream maker. Beat egg
whites; set aside. Mix sugar and egg yolks;
add some milk to dissolve. Add vanilla,
egg whites, more milk and cream last.
Freeze in ice cream freezer.

MAKES ABOUT 1 GALLON

phyllis' ice cream trifle

DANA PARKEY

This is as good as it sounds!

12 to 16 ice cream sandwiches, cut into thirds
1/2 pint whipping cream
1 pint vanilla ice cream
Chocolate sauce in a squeeze bottle
1 cup slivered almonds, toasted
2 ounces Kahlúa

Place your trifle bowl or other glass bowl in
the freezer until chilled. Add a layer of ice
cream sandwiches, whipped topping and ice
cream; drizzle with chocolate sauce and then
sprinkle with almonds and Kahlúa. Repeat
layers until all ingredients are used. Cover
with plastic wrap and freeze until ready
to serve.

BASTILLE DAY

*A French national holiday, Bastille Day commemorates the
storming of the Bastille, which took place on July 14, 1789
and marked the beginning of the French Revolution.*

*Keep the red, white and blue décor from July 4 and turn it
into a tricolour (a French flag, for the uninitiated). Have a
taste-off of French and Texas cheeses and wines...and try
these French-inspired dishes. Bon appétit!*

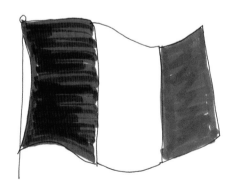

petite jambon et fromage quiches

6 slices of bread
3 eggs
3 tablespoons milk
1/2 cup (heaping) chopped cooked ham
1/2 cup (heading) shredded Gruyère cheese
1 teaspoon Mural of Flavor *or*
    Fox Point Seasoning**
1/8 teaspoon pepper

Preheat oven to 325°. Lightly coat two miniature muffin pans with nonstick cooking spray (wipe out any excess). Remove crust from bread and cut each slice into four squares. Press one bread square into each mini muffin cup (it will line the bottom and go up the sides slightly). In a bowl, beat the eggs; add milk, ham, cheese, seasoning and pepper. Put about 2 teaspoons of egg mixture in each bread cup. Bake for 13-15 minutes or until eggs are set. Quiches will puff up during baking and sink slightly after removing them from the pans.

* These spices are available from Penzeys Spices in the Heights (516 W. 19th Street) or online at penzeys.com.

MAKES 2 DOZEN

tarte de tomate

VERLINDE DOUBLEDAY

1 unbaked pastry shell
1-1/2 cups (6 ounces) shredded
    mozzarella cheese
2 to 4 tablespoons sliced basil leaves
4 to 6 farmers market *or* homegrown
    tomatoes, sliced and seeded
Salt and pepper to taste
Olive oil

Preheat oven to 400°. Cover bottom of pie shell with mozzarella; sprinkle with basil. Top with two layers of sliced tomatoes. Sprinkle with salt and pepper; drizzle with oil. Bake for 30-40 minutes. Cut into wedges.

châteaubriand with spicy hollandaise sauce

KAREN TERRELL

1/2 cup packed light brown sugar

1/4 cup salt

1 beef tenderloin (4 to 5 pounds), trimmed

1/4 cup olive oil

5 egg yolks

1-1/2 cups butter

Juice of 2 lemons

2 teaspoons tomato paste

Cayenne pepper and additional salt

Preheat the oven to 500°. Combine brown sugar and salt; pour onto a baking sheet. Roll the whole tenderloin in the mixture so the meat is completely covered. In a large skillet, heat oil over high heat; cook tenderloin on all sides for 4-6 minutes. Transfer tenderloin to a baking sheet. Finish in the oven for 20-25 minutes or until a meat thermometer reads 140°. Cover with foil and let stand for 10-15 minutes.

While the meat rests, make the sauce. In a food processor fitted with a metal blade, pulse egg yolks on low. Melt butter; while still warm, slowly add to yolks, blending until combined. Add lemon juice and tomato paste while blending. Season to taste with cayenne and salt. Slice beef; serve with sauce.

SERVES 8-10

Wine Recommendation: Becker Reserve Cabernet Sauvignon or Kiepersol Estates Merlot

guillotined chicken with romaine and caper dressing

ANN WALES

3 tablespoons sherry wine vinegar
1/2 cup olive oil
1/4 cup minced shallots
2 tablespoons drained capers
1 tablespoon Dijon mustard
Salt and pepper to taste
4 boneless skinless chicken breasts
  (about 1-3/4 pounds)
2 bunches romaine, halved lengthwise
  with core left intact
Shaved manchego *or* Parmesan cheese,
  optional

To make dressing: Place vinegar, oil, shallots, capers and mustard in a food processor; purée until almost smooth. Season with salt and pepper. Pound chicken to flatten slightly; place in a shallow dish. Pour 1/4 cup dressing over chicken; sprinkle with salt and pepper. Let stand at room temperature for 15 minutes.

Preheat grill to medium-high heat. Place romaine spears, cut side up, on a baking sheet. Drizzle with 1/4 cup dressing and turn to coat. Grill chicken until a meat thermometer reads 170°, about 6 minutes per side. Remove and keep warm. Grill romaine until charred and slightly wilted on all sides, about 2 minutes. Place one chicken breast and one romaine spear on each plate; drizzle with remaining dressing. Sprinkle generously with cheese if desired.

SERVES 4

Wine Recommendation: Brennan Vineyards Viognier
or a Riesling

french green bean casserole

LAURIE LIEDTKE

1 pound fresh green beans *or* haricot verts, trimmed and halved
2 tablespoons butter
1/4 pound mushrooms, roughly chopped
1 clove garlic, minced
1 cup heavy cream
1 cup (4 ounces) shredded Gouda cheese
1/4 to 1/2 cup bread crumbs
Salt and pepper to taste
2 shallots, minced and sautéed

Preheat oven to 350°. Place a 4-quart pot of water over high heat; bring to a boil. Add green beans. When beans are al dente, about 4-5 minutes, drain and cool in an ice-water bath. Drain well once cooled. In a large ovenproof sauté pan, melt butter over medium-high heat; sauté mushrooms and garlic. Add cream; bring to a boil and cook until slightly reduced. Add the beans. Toss in the cheese and bread crumbs. Sprinkle with salt and pepper; stir gently but well. Bake for 15 minutes or until heated through. Cool for a few minutes; top with shallots and serve.

SERVES 4-6

greatest au gratin potatoes

BETTY DAVIS

6 medium red potatoes
1/2 cup plus 1 tablespoon butter, *divided*
1 cup all-purpose flour
1-1/2 teaspoons salt
4 cups milk
2 cups heavy cream *or* half-and-half
1 cup (8 ounces) sour cream
1 cup grated Parmesan cheese
1/2 cup dry bread crumbs

Preheat oven to 375°. Cook potatoes in jackets; peel and cube. In a large saucepan, melt 1/2 cup butter; stir in flour and salt. Scald milk and cream; add to butter mixture, stirring constantly. Cook for 10 minutes. Cool. Add sour cream and potatoes. Pour into a 13-inch x 9-inch x 2-inch glass baking dish. Sprinkle with cheese. Toast bread crumbs in remaining butter; sprinkle over casserole. Bake for 20-30 minutes or until hot and bubbly.

SERVES 4-6

"let them eat..." chocolate cake

ANN WALES

1-3/4 cups all-purpose flour
2 cups sugar
3/4 cup baking cocoa
1 teaspoon salt
1-1/2 teaspoons baking soda
1-1/2 teaspoons baking powder
2 eggs
1 cup whole milk
1/2 cup canola oil
1 teaspoon vanilla extract
1 cup boiling water

Preheat oven to 350°. Combine the flour, sugar, cocoa, salt, baking soda and baking powder; set aside. With a mixer, beat the eggs, milk, oil and vanilla for 4 minutes. Add dry ingredients and beat until combined. Add boiling water; mix well. Pour into two greased 9-inch pans. Bake for 25-30 minutes or until a toothpick comes out clean.

SERVES 12-16

Culinary Lavender is sold at the Bulb and Plant Mart...it is wonderful blended in vanilla ice cream for a taste of Provence.

gâteau au chocolat

RYLAND STACY

1 pound high-quality bittersweet chocolate
1/2 pound unsalted butter, cut into
  small pieces
10 eggs, *separated*
1/4 cup sugar
1/4 cup all-purpose flour
Heavy cream for serving

Preheat oven to 400°. Butter a 10-1/2-inch springform pan. Break chocolate into pieces and melt in the top of a double boiler over boiling water, stirring from time to time. Off the heat, stir butter into melted chocolate until combined. Transfer to a large mixing bowl. In a separate bowl, beat egg whites until they form firm peaks (don't overbeat). In another bowl, whisk yolks and sugar until frothy and lemon-colored; add flour and mix thoroughly. Fold into chocolate mixture. Add one-third of the whites to the batter and blend thoroughly. Very gently fold in the remaining whites. Do this slowly and patiently until no streaks of white remain.

Pour batter into prepared pan. Bake for only 15 minutes. Remove from the oven. Cover the pan with a plate for 12 minutes to keep the cake very moist and supple. Take the plate off and place an unfolded napkin on top until ready to serve. Cake can be made the day before. Serve at room temperature; do not refrigerate. When ready to serve, pour a pool of heavy cream onto dessert plates; slice cake and place on the cream.

SERVES 10-14

crème fraîche

2 tablespoons buttermilk
2 cups heavy cream (not ultra-pasteurized)

Combine and heat until just tepid. Pour into
a clean jar; cover partially and let sit out for
24 hours. Stir; refrigerate for 24 hours more
before you use it. Serve with fresh berries
such as wild strawberries or blueberries.

grand marnier after-dinner drink

RYLAND STACY

*I've enjoyed this drink with Margaret McDermott at her
ranch north of Dallas.*

Finely crushed ice
Juice of a fresh lime
Grand Marnier

Fill a martini glass with finely crushed ice.
Add lime juice and fill to the top with Grand
Marnier. Mix carefully and enjoy.

EXOTIC HOME VACATIONS

*Think of all the "destinations" you can visit without ever
leaving your home. Here are some food ideas to travel to
in your armchair and in your kitchen!*

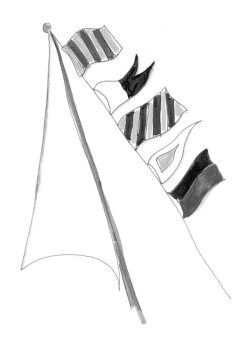

citrus fajita kabobs
MIMI KERR

Juice of 2 oranges
Juice of 1 lime
Juice of 1 lemon
1 teaspoon orange zest
4 cloves garlic, finely chopped
1/4 cup packed brown sugar
Dash of Tabasco
1 flank steak (1-1/2 pounds)
1 yellow bell pepper
1 red bell pepper
1/2 red onion

Polynesian Pool Party

If you can't get away to the Islands, bring the Islands to you. With tiki torches, leis, pineapples, coconuts and tropical recipes like these, you can have a luau by the pool or on the patio.

In a large glass bowl, combine the juices, orange zest, garlic, brown sugar and Tabasco. Remove 1/4 cup to a small bowl; set aside. Slice the flank steak across the grain into thin strips, 1/4 to 1/8 inch thick; add to the marinade in the large bowl and toss to coat. Cover and refrigerate for at least 2 hours. Soak wooden skewers in water for at least 30 minutes.

Cut the bell peppers into 1-inch squares; parboil for 5 minutes. Cut the onion into 1-inch squares and separate. Add to reserved marinade and toss to coat. When ready to cook, preheat the grill to medium. Skewer the steak strips, alternating with pepper and

onion squares. Grill for 3-4 minutes on each side until the meat is nicely and evenly browned. Serve hot with guacamole (recipe on page 44).

SERVES 6

avocado salad with basil

MIMI KERR

2 ripe avocados
1 package (4 ounces) crumbled goat cheese
24 small pitted Niçoise olives
2 tablespoons chopped fresh basil
1/4 cup olive oil
Salt and pepper

Slice one avocado in half lengthwise; with a twisting motion, separate into halves. Remove the seed with a spoon. Carefully scoop out the entire avocado half by sliding your thumb between the skin and the fruit. Place cut side down and slice into narrow crescents. Fan avocado slices out on a serving plate. Repeat with remaining avocado. Sprinkle goat cheese, olives and basil over avocado slices. Drizzle with oil. Season lightly with salt and generously with pepper. Serve immediately.

SERVES 4

pool party decorations ~ mimi kerr

Here are some ideas for a luau party or any seaside themed gathering:

* "Plant" wildflowers or daisies in tiki cups.
* Cover a table with a cloth or use a straw beach mat as a runner. In the middle, mound brown sugar or play sand. Press some of the brown sugar into sand molds and invert. Add seashells, toy boats, sunglasses, bottles of sunscreen, cocktail umbrellas, and little shovels and pails. The ideas are endless!
* Cut the top off a fresh pineapple, 1 inch from the top, and hollow out from the top. Fill the pineapple "vase" with water; add flowers inserted in crazy straws.
* Fill votives with sand and add candles.

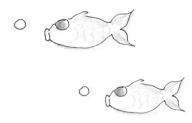

light baked salmon

SHELBY JONES

Deep-Sea Fishing in Alaska

Salmon is king in the 49th state, but if you can't travel all the way north, you can catch some fish at the market and enjoy it at home. The pepper and onion salad salutes the giant vegetables grown in the "Land of the Midnight Sun."

1 salmon fillet (1 pound)
1/2 cup light soy sauce
1/4 cup Splenda brown sugar blend *or*
   1/2 cup regular brown sugar
2 tablespoons olive oil
2 tablespoons lemon juice
3/4 teaspoon garlic powder
1/2 teaspoon pepper

Place salmon in a shallow glass dish. Combine the remaining ingredients; pour over salmon. Place in the refrigerator to marinate for 2 hours. Preheat oven to 350°. Bake, uncovered, for 30 minutes or until fish flakes with a fork.

SERVES 2-4

Wine Recommendation: Chardonnay

sweet piquant peppers

GAIL HENDRYX

Serve this warm as a side dish, at room temperature for a summer salad, as an addition to a salad or as an antipasto. Topped with a piece of grilled salmon or a skewer of shrimp, it makes a wonderful dinner. If you don't like heat, leave out the poblano. If you prefer crispy veggies, don't cook them as long, but the vinegar/sweetener becomes more of a dressing than a glaze. The longer the vinegar has been aged, the less sweetener you will need.

2 to 3 tablespoons olive oil
2 red bell peppers, julienned
2 yellow bell peppers, julienned
2 orange bell peppers, julienned
1 poblano pepper, seeded and thinly sliced
1 jumbo sweet onion, thinly sliced
4 cloves garlic, smashed, peeled and
   coarsely chopped
1/2 teaspoon kosher salt
1/4 to 1/2 teaspoon crushed red pepper flakes
1 to 2 tablespoons balsamic vinegar
   (aged preferred)
Freshly ground pepper to taste
1/2 teaspoon Splenda *or* sugar to taste

Heat a large frying pan over medium heat; add oil. Add the peppers, onion, garlic and salt. Let the mixture cook down until there is no crispness left in the vegetables and they have just begun to caramelize. Depending upon the size of the pan and the water content of the vegetables, this could take 30-40 minutes. Add more oil during the cooking process if sticking occurs. While veggies are cooking, add the pepper flakes. When desired consistency is achieved, stir in the vinegar, ground pepper and sweetener. Cook just until vinegar coats all the vegetables and sweetener is dissolved.

MAKES 3 CUPS

raj appetizer

CHER KHAN

I package (8 ounces) cream cheese,
  close to room temperature
4 tablespoons milk *or* cream
3/4 teaspoon curry powder
Chutney to cover
3/4 cup roasted salted peanuts
1/4 cup chopped green onion tops

Soften cream cheese with the milk; add curry powder and mix well. Spread on a serving plate to about 3/4 inch thick. Refrigerate. When ready to serve, cover cheese spread with chutney; sprinkle with peanuts and green onion tops. Serve with crackers.

SERVES 8-10

Song of India Soirée

Nothing is more delicious than exotic foods—curries, hot pepper dishes and cooling dips naturally go with warm weather. For dessert, serve chilled sliced mangoes with a sprinkling of lemon juice and zest. Have a feast without leaving the country!

Give old flowerpots new life: Clean them out well and then use paint from the hardware store or craft store to add a splash of color indoors or out.

caroline's tandoori chicken drumsticks

LUCY GOODRICH

1-1/2 cups whole plain yogurt
1/4 cup vegetable oil
8 teaspoons tandoori masala
  seasoning powder
16 chicken drumsticks
1/2 cup chopped fresh cilantro

Mix the yogurt, oil and tandoori masala;
coat the chicken with this mixture. Marinate
overnight if possible in the refrigerator.
Preheat oven to 350°. Transfer drumsticks,
lightly blotting one at a time to prevent sauce
from burning, to a baking sheet or pan. Bake
on a lower rack for about 30 minutes. Then
baste with oil and broil until browned. Serve
drumsticks piled high like a bonfire. Garnish
with cilantro.

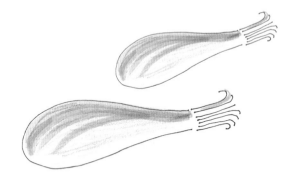

Wine Recommendation: a dry Riesling

*Yogurt mixed with mint and a dash of cumin
is a nice addition to the tandoori drumsticks
or lamb curry.*

lamb curry

DELBY WILLINGHAM

1/2 cup butter
2 large onions, sliced
3 large cloves garlic, crushed
1 tablespoon ground coriander
1 teaspoon ground ginger
3/4 teaspoon ground cumin
1/2 teaspoon ground cinnamon
1/4 teaspoon red pepper
1/4 teaspoon ground turmeric
2 pounds lamb, cut into small pieces
2 cups chicken broth
Salt to taste
Hot cooked basmati rice

condiment suggestions:

Grated or flaked coconut, toasted
Chopped chives
Grated orange and lemon peel
Green onion rounds
Slivered almonds, browned in butter
Chopped peanuts
Crumbled cooked bacon
Raisins soaked in port or vermouth
Minced avocado sprinkled with lemon
Chopped hard-boiled egg
Fried bananas sprinkled with
    cinnamon and cloves

Chutney
Pitted ripe olives
Chopped green olives
Chopped candied ginger

Melt butter in a large pot. Add onions and garlic; cook over medium heat until onions brown. Add spices and sauté for 3 minutes. Add lamb; sauté for 10 minutes. Add broth and salt. Keep heat low and cook until meat is tender, 1-1/2 to 2 hours. If needed, add more water or broth. Serve hot on basmati rice with your choice of condiments.

Wine Recommendation: Shiraz or Zinfandel

coronation chicken

CARL ESTES

When Princess Elizabeth suddenly became Queen in 1953, rations were still scarce in the United Kingdom after the war. Constance Spry invented this recipe from staples readily available. We had it in Morocco and were besotted. Serve with Pimm's Cup. The sun never sets on the Empire!

1 tablespoon olive oil

1/4 cup slivered almonds

1 tablespoon vegetable oil

1/2 small yellow onion, chopped

1/4 to 1/2 teaspoon mild curry powder

1/4 cup chicken stock

Juice of 1/4 lemon

1 tablespoon apricot jam

1/2 teaspoon tomato purée

1/2 cup mayonnaise

1-1/2 tablespoons heavy cream

2 chicken breasts, cooked and cut into
 bite-size pieces

8 seedless green grapes, quartered

Heat the olive oil in a small skillet; toast almonds until they begin to turn golden. Drain and set aside until serving. In a small saucepan, heat the vegetable oil; add onion and sauté gently until soft but not brown. Stir in the curry powder; cook for 2 minutes (this will help bring out the flavor). Add the stock, lemon juice, jam and tomato purée. Cook and stir until bubbling, then cook for 5 more minutes until the mixture reduces and thickens. Cool for 30 minutes or so, then stir in the mayonnaise and cream. If making a day ahead, stop here and refrigerate the sauce, chicken, grapes and almonds separately. The next day, warm up the sauce; add the chicken and mix to warm thoroughly. Serve over cold rice. Garnish with toasted almonds and quartered grapes.

SERVES 4

coconut mousse with mango sauce

PAULE JOHNSTON

Make this the day before. Instead of serving with the mango sauce, you can purchase butterscotch sauce.

2 cups cold milk, *divided*
1 cup sugar (less if using sweetened coconut)
1/4 teaspoon salt
2 tablespoons unflavored gelatin
1 pint heavy cream, whipped stiff
2 cups freshly grated coconut*
1 teaspoon vanilla extract *or* liqueur of choice

sauce:

1 jar of mangoes (cold or canned)
Lemon juice
Finely grated lemon peel

Heat 1-1/2 cups milk with sugar and salt; cool slightly. In a bowl, dissolve gelatin in remaining cold milk. Stir in hot milk mixture. Put in refrigerator until it starts to thicken, then beat until fluffy and light. Fold in whipped cream. Fold in coconut. Add vanilla or liqueur. Pour into a melon mold; refrigerate until firm. Just before serving, blend the sauce ingredients. Carefully unmold mousse in the center of serving plate, with sauce in center.

* *Coconut powder is my favorite (found in Asian stores); packaged coconut is fine, but it is heavier.*

sangria pedro romero

LADY BRETT ASHLEY

A Spanish red wine, such as a Rioja, would be perfect in this drink.

1 lemon
1 orange
1 lime
1/4 cup superfine sugar
4 ounces brandy *or* orange liqueur
1 bottle (750 ml) red wine
2 tablespoons lemon juice
1 bottle (10 ounces) soda water
Ice cubes

Slice the lemon, orange and lime; place in a large pitcher. Add sugar and brandy; slightly muddle the fruit. Let stand for 1 hour. Stir in the wine and lemon juice. Let stand again. Just before serving, add soda water and ice. Stir and serve very cold.

Costa del Sol Siesta

Let your imagination take you to Spain's Costa del Sol, with exotic Tangier just across the Mediterranean—sandy beaches and millionaires' villas all around. For a taste of the local cuisine, enjoy blood orange juice (which you can now obtain fresh from the supermarket) with a splash of Champagne or relax with a traditional sangria. Marcona almonds, which taste like none other, are the perfect complement.

chicken alhambra

LYDIA HILLIARD

Serve with fresh bread and a fresh orange salad (try Clementine Salad on page 79). For dessert, Spanish cheeses or sliced oranges marinated in Jerez (Spanish sherry) would be a nice complement.

1 package (12 ounces) apricots
1 jar (3.5 ounces) capers, drained
1 cup drained black Spanish olives
1/2 cup red wine vinegar
1/2 cup olive oil
6 bay leaves
2 cloves garlic, minced
1 tablespoon dried oregano
1 tablespoon coarse sea salt
2 teaspoons pepper
8 pounds skinned mixed chicken pieces
1 cup brown sugar (or less to taste)
1 cup dry white wine
1/4 cup chopped fresh parsley

Combine the first 10 ingredients in one or two large ziplock freezer bags or large bowls. Add chicken pieces, turning to coat well. Seal or cover and refrigerate overnight, turning occasionally.

Preheat oven to 350°. Arrange chicken pieces in a single layer in two 13-inch x 9-inch x 2-inch baking pans. Pour marinade over chicken; sprinkle evenly with brown sugar. Pour wine around chicken. Bake for 45-60 minutes, basting frequently. Remove chicken, prunes, olives and capers to a serving platter. Discard bay leaves. Drizzle pan juices over chicken; sprinkle with parsley. Serve with rice or pasta.

SERVES 8

Wine Recommendation: Sauvignon Blanc

"It is impossible to think anything but pleasant thoughts while eating a fresh homegrown tomato."

~Lewis Grizzard, American writer and humorist

bayou tomato soup

VERLINDE DOUBLEDAY

An oldie but not seen around much anymore. You can lightly whirl the tomatoes in a food processor rather than chopping them if you prefer. A chilled soup is refreshing on a hot summer day!

6 cups tomatoes, peeled, seeded and
   very finely chopped
1 medium sweet onion, grated
3/4 cup lemon juice
1 teaspoon vinegar
1 teaspoon celery seed
Salt to taste
6 tablespoons mayonnaise
1 tablespoon chopped fresh parsley
1/4 teaspoon curry powder
Small parsley sprigs for garnish

In a large bowl, combine tomatoes, onion, lemon juice, vinegar and celery seed; mix well. Season with salt. Pour into a freezer tray and freeze to a mush, about 1 hour. In a small bowl, combine the mayonnaise, chopped parsley and curry powder. Serve the soup half frozen, topped with seasoned mayonnaise and garnished with a parsley sprig.

SERVES 6

Wish You Were in Dixie?

The "land of cotton" is the inspiration for this collection of old favorites from the Deep South.

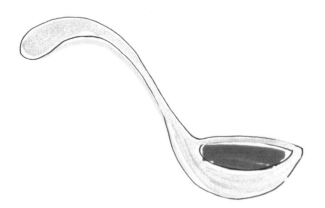

southern shrimp and cheese grits

SHELBY JONES

1 cup quick-cooking grits
1/4 cup unsalted butter
1-1/4 cups shredded extra sharp
   cheddar cheese
1/2 teaspoon Tabasco
1/4 teaspoon cayenne pepper
1/4 teaspoon paprika
1/4 teaspoon Worcestershire sauce
1/2 teaspoon salt
1/8 teaspoon pepper

shrimp and sauce:

4 to 5 bacon strips
1 tablespoon olive oil
1 tablespoon minced garlic
1-1/4 pounds shrimp, peeled and deveined
1-1/4 cups chicken broth
1/2 cup white wine
3 tablespoons lemon juice
2 tablespoons all-purpose flour
1/4 cup cold water
1/4 teaspoon Kitchen Bouquet
1 bunch green onions, chopped

Cook grits according to package directions. Add the butter, cheese and seasonings. Keep warm until serving time.

In a large skillet, cook bacon until crisp. Crumble bacon and set aside, reserving drippings. Add oil to bacon drippings; heat over medium-high. Add garlic and sauté briefly. Add shrimp; cook until they're pink and cooked through. Remove shrimp and keep warm. Add broth, wine and lemon juice to the cooking juices; bring to a boil. Mix flour and cold water until smooth; add to the hot liquid, stirring constantly until thickened. Add Kitchen Bouquet.

When ready to serve, add 2-3 tablespoons of milk to grits if needed for desired consistency. Spoon grits into individual serving bowls or onto plates. Top with shrimp and sauce; sprinkle with crumbled bacon and chopped green onions.

SERVES 6-8

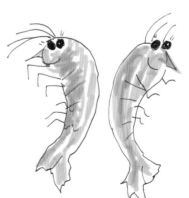

summer squash casserole

GAIL ANDERSON

10 medium yellow summer squash, sliced
1 yellow onion, chopped
1 to 2 tablespoons vegetable oil
6 eggs, lightly beaten
1 tablespoon sugar
1/2 teaspoon salt
1/2 teaspoon pepper
40 saltines, crushed
3 tablespoons butter, melted

Preheat oven to 350° (325° if using a glass baking dish). Drop squash into a small amount of boiling water; cover and cook until crisp-tender, about 15 minutes. Drain very well; place in a large bowl. Sauté onion in oil. Add onion, eggs, sugar, salt and pepper to squash; mix well. Transfer to a greased 13-inch x 9-inch x 2-inch baking dish. Sprinkle with crushed crackers; drizzle with butter. Bake, uncovered, for 30-35 minutes.

SERVES 8-10

nanny's strawberry shortcake with special custard topping

GAIL ANDERSON

1 cup sugar
1 teaspoon sifted flour
1 egg, well beaten
1 cup water
1 tablespoon butter
1 teaspoon vanilla extract (or to taste)
1 box of Bisquick
4 cups well-sugared strawberries

Make the custard in a double boiler. Combine sugar and flour; add to egg and continue beating until light and fluffy. Heat water with butter; add sugar and egg mixture, stirring until it is a smooth, creamy custard. Add vanilla. Follow directions on box of Bisquick for shortcakes. Split warm shortcakes; top with strawberries and custard.

SERVES 6

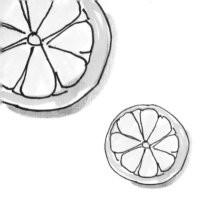

high island iced tea

This is the classic Long Island Iced Tea, but we like to call it High Island after the coastal town not far from Galveston. It's potent, so handle with care!

1 part vodka
1 part tequila
1 part rum
1 part gin
1 part Triple Sec
1-1/2 parts sweet and sour mix
Splash of Coca-Cola

Mix ingredients together over ice in a glass. Pour into a shaker and give one brisk shake. Pour back into the glass; garnish with a lemon or lime wedge or slice.

At the Shore

No plane fare nor rental cottage required…a trip to the local farmers market and fish market are as far as you'll need to go to make these fresh summer salads, delightful muffins and succulent seafood dishes. And make sure your bar is stocked to make this famous cocktail. Go coastal, not postal!

gulf coast
shrimp salad

DODIE JACKSON

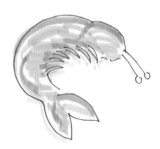

1/2 cup plus 2 tablespoons white wine
   vinegar, *divided*
5 teaspoons sea salt, *divided*
5-1/2 pounds large shrimp,
   peeled and deveined
1 cup olive oil
1 teaspoon minced garlic
1/2 teaspoon fresh thyme leaves
Zest of 2 lemons
1/4 cup freshly squeezed lemon juice
1 teaspoon Dijon mustard
1/2 teaspoon freshly ground pepper
3/4 cup diced celery
3 tablespoons chopped fresh parsley
2 lemons, thinly sliced for garnish

Fill a large pot with 2 quarts of water; add
1/2 cup vinegar and 3 teaspoons sea salt.
Bring to a boil. Add shrimp and cook for
only 2 minutes. Remove from the heat and
drain; place shrimp in a large serving bowl.

In a medium sauté pan, heat oil; add garlic,
thyme and lemon zest. Cook over low heat
for about 1 minute. Remove from the heat;
add the lemon juice, mustard, pepper and
remaining vinegar and sea salt. Pour the hot
mixture over the shrimp. Add the celery and
parsley and toss well. Garnish with lemon
slices. This salad can be served immediately,
but it is best when allowed to sit for an
hour first.

SERVES 12

Wine Recommendation: Fall Creek Sauvignon Blanc

catalina salad

KATHY LOVE

6 asparagus spears, trimmed and cut into
   1-inch pieces
1 bunch *or* bag fresh baby spinach
2 avocados, cut into pieces
2 apples, peeled and diced
1 pint fresh blueberries (can use
   dried blueberries)
5 thick slices of bacon, cooked and crumbled
3/4 cup walnut pieces, toasted
1/2 cup crumbled blue cheese

dressing:

1/4 cup lemon juice
1 tablespoon hot Chinese mustard
1 teaspoon Cholula hot sauce
3/4 cup olive oil

Blanch the asparagus pieces and plunge
in ice water to cool. In a salad bowl, toss
the spinach, avocados, apples, blueberries,
bacon, walnuts, blue cheese and asparagus.
In a jar, shake the lemon juice, mustard
and hot sauce. Add oil and shake well. Pour
desired amount of dressing over salad (just
lightly coat; there may be some left over).

louie louie salad

GAY ESTES

*For a great summertime meal, compose a crab "Louie
Louie!" Serve it with Real Man's Thousand Island
Dressing, buy some sourdough bread and open a frosty
beer. For a variation, use fresh shrimp instead of crab.*

1 head iceberg lettuce
Fresh cooked crabmeat
Sliced avocados, tomatoes and
   hard-boiled eggs

real man's thousand island dressing:

1 cup mayonnaise
1 tablespoon minced fresh parsley
1 tablespoon chopped drained sweet pickle *or*
   1 tablespoon chopped drained green olives
1 hard-boiled egg, finely chopped, optional
1 tablespoon drained capers
1 teaspoon minced shallot
1 teaspoon lemon juice (or to taste)
1/4 teaspoon Dijon mustard
Salt and pepper to taste

Slice the head of lettuce into eight wedges,
or shred to make a bed of lettuce; place on
salad plates. Arrange the crab, avocados,
tomatoes and eggs over lettuce. In a small
bowl, combine the dressing ingredients.
Serve on the side.

SERVES 8

texas blueberry muffins

MARGARET GRIFFITH

1 cup milk
1/2 cup unsalted butter
1-1/2 teaspoons grated orange peel
1 teaspoon vanilla extract
2 eggs
2 cups all-purpose flour
3/4 cup sugar
2-1/2 teaspoons baking powder
3/4 teaspoon salt
1-1/3 cups fresh *or* frozen blueberries

Preheat oven to 400°. Combine the milk, butter, orange peel and vanilla in a small heavy saucepan; stir over medium heat until butter melts. Cool until mixture is warm to the touch. Beat in eggs. Sift flour, sugar, baking powder and salt into a large bowl. Add milk mixture and stir just until blended. Fold in blueberries (if using frozen berries, do not thaw). Divide batter among 12 paper-lined or greased muffin cups. Bake for 20 minutes or until golden and a tester inserted into center of muffins comes out clean. Transfer to a wire rack.

MAKES 1 DOZEN

salmon with horseradish and tarragon topping

LESLYE WEAVER

1 cup light mayonnaise
1/4 cup dry bread crumbs
2 tablespoons cream-style horseradish
2 tablespoons chopped chives
1-1/2 teaspoons dill weed
1 teaspoon Dijon mustard
1/2 teaspoon dried tarragon
Juice of 1 lemon
Salt and pepper to taste
Salmon fillets

Preheat oven to 375°. Blend all ingredients except for the fish. Spread the mixture evenly over the top of the salmon. Place in a shallow baking dish. This can be done several hours before baking; refrigerate if not baking immediately. Bake for 20 minutes or until salmon flakes easily with a fork.

top-of-stove easy summer shrimp newburg

GAIL ANDERSON

2 tablespoons butter
1-3/4 tablespoons all-purpose flour
1 cup heavy cream
3 tablespoons ketchup
3/4 tablespoon Worcestershire sauce
1 pound small cooked shrimp
A few grains of cayenne pepper
Salt and pepper to taste
2 tablespoons sherry

In a saucepan, melt butter; stir in flour until blended. Gradually add cream. When the sauce is thick, stir in ketchup and Worcestershire sauce. Add shrimp and stir until they are heated through. Add seasonings to taste. Just before serving, add sherry. Serve over rice or toast points.

SERVES 4

baked tilapia

SHELBY JONES

Grouper, trout or other whitefish work just as well in this recipe.

1 medium green bell pepper, chopped
1 medium onion, chopped
Salt and pepper
4 tilapia fillets
1-1/2 to 2 teaspoons Worcestershire sauce
1/4 cup freshly grated Parmesan cheese
  (or to taste)

Preheat oven to 350°. Set aside 1/4 cup green pepper for topping. Sprinkle onion and remaining green pepper over the bottom of a casserole dish. Rub a small amount of salt and pepper into each tilapia fillet; place on top of onion and green pepper. Sprinkle with Worcestershire sauce. Bake for 20 minutes or until fish is firm and opaque. Sprinkle with Parmesan and reserved green pepper. Return to the oven until cheese melts.

SERVES 4

Wine Recommendation: Sauvignon Blanc

Happy Campers

A day of swimming, horseback riding, tennis, naptime, dinner and a show…can we go back, please? We promise to write a letter once a week!

waldemar corn and goat cheese casserole

MEG TAPP

When the Garden Club went on a field trip to Camp Waldemar, a girls camp near Hunt that's been in operation since 1926, we were served this for lunch. Everyone had seconds!

1 small onion, chopped
1 small green bell pepper, chopped
1 cup unsalted butter
2 eggs, beaten
1 can (15.25 ounces) whole kernel corn
   with juice
1 can (14.75 ounces) creamed corn
1 can (4 ounces) chopped green chiles
1 package (4 ounces) crumbled goat cheese
1 cup chopped fresh cilantro
1 teaspoon ground cumin
1/2 teaspoon salt
1 package (16 ounces) cornbread mix
2 cups (8 ounces) shredded Mexican
   cheese blend

Preheat oven to 375°. Sauté onion and green pepper in butter until tender. In a large bowl, mix the eggs, corn with juice, creamed corn, chiles, goat cheese, cilantro, cumin and salt. Stir in cornbread mix and sautéed

vegetables. Spoon into a greased 13-inch x
9-inch x 2-inch baking pan. Sprinkle shredded cheese on top. Bake, uncovered, for 30
minutes or until firm.

SERVES 10-12

*Wine Recommendation: Messina Hof
unoaked Chardonnay*

kick the can ice cream

MIKKI PHILLIPS

*What could be better on a summer day than making
homemade ice cream? Maybe a game of kick the can?*

3 cups heavy cream
3/4 cup milk
3/4 cup sugar
3/4 cup egg substitute
1/2 teaspoon vanilla extract
2 coffee cans (one 1-pound and one
   3-pound) with plastic lids
Crushed ice
3/4 cup rock salt, *divided*
Masking tape
Waffle bowls *or* cones, optional
Candy-coated milk chocolate
   sprinkles, optional

Stir together the cream, milk, sugar,
egg substitute and vanilla; pour into the
1-pound coffee can. Seal with lid; place
inside the 3-pound coffee can. Fill large
can with ice and half of the rock salt. Secure
small can in place with masking tape. Seal
large can with lid. Roll large can with your
foot for 5 minutes. Remove lid from large
can and drain off water. Add more ice and
remaining rock salt. Replace lid and roll
can for 10 minutes. Let stand for 5 minutes
before serving. Ice cream will be soft. If
desired, serve in waffle bowls or cones
and decorate with chocolate sprinkles.

MAKES 3 CUPS

SPA DAY

Not going anywhere, and the summer heat is innervating? Treat yourself
at home with these pick-me-ups. No humans or animals were harmed
during the testing of these recipes.

go and grow greener juice

3 to 4 carrots
2 to 3 apples
1-inch slice of peeled fresh gingerroot

Put through a juicer; drink this great-tasting juice. Use the pulp for muffins or quick breads such as zucchini or banana-nut bread.

skin and body tonic

Fix yourself a beautiful pitcher of ice and water. Add any fresh fruit on hand: a few strawberries, melon slices, lemon or lime slices, fresh mint, even cucumbers. Makes a great-tasting flavored water and looks pretty in a pitcher.

sugar facial

Mix 1 cup sugar with 1/4 cup canola or light vegetable oil. Keep in a jar and apply to your face twice a week; rub gently and avoid your eyes. Wash off and apply moisturizer.

sugar scrub

Soap your face and lather with your favorite soap. Place 1/4 teaspoon sugar in your palm and slowly rub into the lather in circles. Rinse thoroughly and apply moisturizer.

oatmeal brown sugar facial scrub

Oatmeal is hypoallergenic and full of amino acids that nourish and moisturize the skin. Oatmeal is perfect for people with sensitive skin, as it is a natural anti-inflammatory, it gently exfoliates and cleans, and soothes dry itchy skin.

Brown sugar contains a number of the finest oils from all over the world, and for that reason is used as a natural moisturizer in many skin-care products. Brown sugar will rejuvenate skin while gently removing dead skin cells.

Aloe vera is famous for soothing burns, but it is also a gentle cleansing agent and moisturizer. Be sure that you purchase 100% aloe vera gel or squeeze the aloe directly from a live plant.

Lemon is a natural gentle astringent that will help to clear and refine pores and eliminate acne without overdrying the skin. If you have oily skin, add an extra teaspoon of lemon juice to the mix.

2 tablespoons oats
2 tablespoons brown sugar
2 tablespoons aloe vera
1 teaspoon lemon juice

Grind the oats in a blender or food processor; place in a medium bowl. Add brown sugar, aloe vera and lemon juice. Stir until the mixture has an even, creamy consistency. Apply the scrub to damp skin and gently massage.

hair and scalp cocktail

NORA WATSON

2 tablespoons vodka
2 tablespoons honey
1/2 ripe avocado
1 egg yolk

Blend or mash all ingredients until creamy.
Apply to shampooed head for 30 minutes.
Rinse well. Lightly shampoo.

*Variation: Rinse your hair in vinegar in which you have
placed fresh rosemary. It will smell divine and give your
hair a shine. Try with lavender as well.*

herbal bath soak

Place 5 sprigs of fresh rosemary or 1/4 cup
dried lavender and/or dried rose petals
on a double thickness of cheesecloth; tie
with string to form a bag and add to 1
box of Epsom salts. Place in a lidded glass
container. Remove the cheesecloth bag
after 2 weeks. Pour 1 cup of the salts into
a tub of hot water; let sit for 10 minutes
before bathing. You may create your own
mix of herbs and scents. The salts make a
nice gift in an attractive jar.

garden
glossary

rose tea

LUCY GOODRICH

*Roses love this mixture once a week, once a
month...anytime. You can find these ingredients at
Southwest Fertilizer on Bissonnet here in Houston.*

2 to 3 tablespoons alfalfa pellets
2 to 3 tablespoons fish emulsion
2 to 3 tablespoons Epsom salts

Place the ingredients in a recycled 1-gallon
milk container. Fill with water. Let sit
outside for several days in the heat and sun.
Shake before pouring a pint to a quart at
the base of each rosebush.

*Roses are fragile. When using in an arrangement,
dethorn carefully to prevent the head from drooping.
Keep them away from apples, as roses are "allergic"
to them; the ethane gas emitted by the apples
ages the flowers.*

hummingbird plants

Ruby-throated hummers migrate through Houston typically in August and September and again in April, feeding like crazy to fatten up for the long flights. They often mate here in April. Try these plants in your garden to attract those lovely little birds.

Aniscanthus
Bleeding heart
Buddleia
Bulbine
Butterfly weed
Caesalpina
Cape honeysuckle lonicera
Cat's whiskers
Clerodendron
Columbine
Coral bean
Crab apple
Crossvine
Cuphea
Firespike
Hamelia
Joe-pye weed
Lantana
Louisiana iris
Penstemon
Pentas
Rosemary
Russelia

Salvia coccinea
Silverbell
Tecoma stans
Terri's pink hibiscus
Turk's cap
Vitex

plants that repel garden pests

DODIE JACKSON

Basil: tomato worms
Catnip: ants, fleas and mosquitoes
Chives: aphids (plant among roses and lettuces)
Lavender: slugs
Marigolds: plant throughout your garden, as pests hate the scent
Mint: aphids, cabbage moths, cabbage worms
Nasturtium: aphids and whiteflies
Onion: ants
Oregano: cucumber beetles
Pennyroyal: ants and fleas
Petunias: aphids and leafhoppers
Rosemary: cabbage moths and bean beetles
Thyme: cabbage worms and slugs

native plants for upper gulf coast area

Shrubs
American beautyberry
Mock-orange
Oakleaf hydrangea
Southern wax myrtle
Sweetshrub
Yaupon

Trees
American holly
Carolina silverbell
Fringe tree
Flowering dogwood
Redbird
Red buckeye
Yaupon holly

Vines
Carolina jasmine
Clematis virginiana (virgin's bower)
Coral honeysuckle
Crossvine
Trumpet creeper

Wildflowers
Bee balm
Black-eyed Susan
Blazing star
Butterfly weed
Cardinal flower
Indian blanket-gaillardia pulchella
Purple coneflower
Tickseed coreopsis
Sunflower helianthus

scents in the garden

Alyssum
Angel trumpet
Anise
Banana shrub
Cape honeysuckle lonicera
Chaste tree (vitex)
Citrus
Crinum
Daisy gardenia
"Ducher" Rose
Ginger
Jasmine
LA lilies
Lemon verbena
Mint
Nicotiana
Night-blooming jasmine or cereus
Old man's beard clematis
Passion vine "incense"
Pineapple guava
Rosemary
Sweet olive
Virginia sweetspire
Yesterday, today and tomorrow

be green: go greener!

* Start a tiny compost pile in a corner of your backyard. Only compost waste; nothing with oil or fat.

* Toss leftover coffee or tea, used coffee grounds or tea leaves, banana peels (around roses especially) and eggshells in the garden.

* If pine trees grow in your yard, use pine straw as azalea and camellia mulch. It's the best!

* Use shredded newspaper as mulch in your garden.

* Newspapers are also good for cleaning mirrors and windows.

* Cut down on the use of personal disposable water bottles or eliminate completely.

* Don't overload the clothes dryer, and clean the lint trap after every use because of the fire hazard. A clothesline is an excellent option.

* Use rags rather than paper towels…use paper towels sparingly.

* Put outdoor lights on timers, and use lower wattages whenever possible.

* Encourage yard crews to use rakes and brooms instead of leaf blowers. Your neighbors will bless you.

* Pick up after your dog. Dog waste biodegrades slowly, and if it's not picked up, it washes into the storm drains and into our waterways, which eventually runs into our water supply.

* Store a canvas shopping bag in your car filled with other canvas and netted shopping bags rolled up for using at the grocery store.

* Central Market recycles plastic bags of all kinds: produce, grocery, dry cleaning, etc. Just place them in the hamper by the check out area—so easy. What good neighbors!

* Save paper by registering for electronic newsletters and info of all kinds, and banking online. If you do not really need a receipt, tell the clerk to help the retailer save paper.

* Take used printer ink cartridges to be recycled or refilled. One such place that does this is Cartridge World (with three locations in Houston). You'll save money and help the environment at the same time.

* When purchasing new electronic devices of all kinds (televisions, computer monitors, cell phones), inquire if the store recycles or where can you take old equipment to be recycled.

recipe index

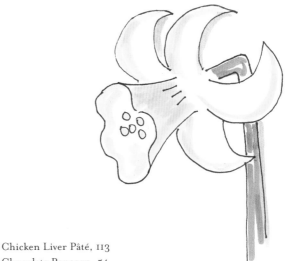

S

sources and bibliography

aggiehort@tamu.edu
Bulb and Plant Mart Guide, The Garden Club of Houston
Church Ladies Guide to Divine Flower Arranging, Gay Estes,
    Bright Sky Press
Does It Come in Green?, Stony Brook Garden Club
Earth Friendly Alternatives, Stonington Garden Club,
    Stonington, Connecticut
Florists' Review Magazine Design School
Flower Decoration, Constance Spry
Green Clean: The Environmentally Sound Guide to Cleaning Your Home,
    Linda Mason Hunter and Mikki Halpin,
    Melcher Media
Houston Chronicle, HoustonGrows.com calendar
Perennial Favorites, The Garden Club of Houston,
    Bright Sky Press
Some Like It Hot—Flowers That Thrive in Hot Humid Weather,
    P.J. Gartin, Wyrick & Company